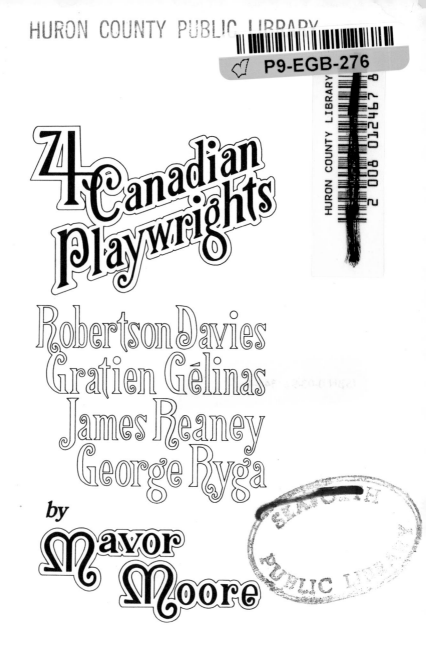

4 Canadian Playwrights

Robertson Davies
Gratien Gélinas
James Reaney
George Ryga

by
Mavor Moore

Holt, Rinehart & Winston of Canada, Limited
Toronto   Montreal

Distributed in the United States of America by
Winston Press, Minneapolis

ISBN 0-03-929990-2

Distributed in the United States of America by
Winston Press,
25 Groveland Terrace,
Minneapolis, Minnesota 55403.

Published simultaneously in Great Britain by
Holt-Blond, Limited,
120 Golden Lane,
Barbican,
London E.C. 1Y OTU, England.

Printed in Canada

1   2   3   4   5   77   76   75   74   73

Contents

Foreword

The present volume is intended primarily as an introduction to the ideas and the work of a few contemporary writers for the Canadian theatre. It is addressed to the general reader as well as the student, to those in Canada and outside of it who wish to know more about our theatre and our playwrights, to those fortunate enough to be able to go to the theatre often, and to those who would like to go more often than they can.

The form it takes, however, may need a brief explanation —for this is neither a quartet of biographies, a critical assessment, nor an anthology of plays. Biographies of our playwrights may be found in such works as the *Oxford Companion to Canadian History and Literature,* (Toronto: Oxford University Press), *Creative Canadians* (Victoria: University of Victoria Press), or the forthcoming *Contemporary Dramatists* (London: St. James Press). As for criticism either scholarly or journalistic, we have perhaps suffered in this country from one extreme or the other: on the one hand, lofty put-downs by pedants who mistakenly judge drama as literature; on the other, hasty "notices" from dabblers too often incapable of grasping what the author was trying to do, what the director and cast did to or for him, and the difference between the two. We have also been subjected to the Judas-kiss of the chauvinist, who wants desperately to discover a Canadian Ibsen tomorrow but wouldn't know him if he met him. As for anthologies, some are noted in our bibliography, and more are appearing regularly.

I have wanted, rather, to fill in a serious gap. In my own classes at York University I have found that most students, raised on British, American and European drama and films and relatively unfamiliar with Canadian plays, tend to regard the latter patronizingly at first as failed attempts to be à la mode. They are not prepared, that is to say, to grant merit to what may in fact be an author's most distinctive and original achievement: the ways in which his approach differs from what has been aptly called the International Fellowship Style. The Canadian playwright is too often measured by how well he stacks up against writers reflecting other societies, and not by how penetratingly or skilfully he deals with his own.

This injustice is magnified by the likelihood that the student will have read more plays than he has seen, and that those he has read will be the masterpieces of world literature. Double jeopardy, this: his value-judgements will be literary rather than theatrical, and he will be comparing apples and oranges. The only way to judge a play properly is in a theatre, just as the only way to judge a symphony is not from the score but in performance; and the main justification for reading plays is that the lack of opportunity to see them produced should not rob us of the lesser pleasure of imagining a production. To "read" a playscript takes quite as much skill as to "read" a musical score, however; and students need less literary analysis and much more creative theatrical guidance than they have been getting. As for the jeopardy of comparing our recent and modest output with the accumulated masterworks of mankind, it is important not to fall into the trap—common a decade ago when the best of literature was compared to the worst of television to prove the former's superiority—of classifying Art into the Golden Ages of Others. Salutary as it may be to measure oneself against the giants, it may also have the effect, so pervasive in Canada, of persuading one that there is little use in trying.

Even the advice to go straight ahead and see or read the plays seems, however, to be insufficient for many Canadian students, theatre-goers and drama buffs. Precisely because they so often begin by looking for values which are intentionally not there, they miss the values which *are* there—unless some of them are pointed out in advance. Naturally this does not mean that they will necessarily like the plays, only that they may understand them better and may be *prepared* to like them—or to dislike them with better reason.

With these considerations in mind, I have included here short essays designed to alert the reader to the individual aims, qualities and methods of each of our authors. There are only four playwrights represented in this book, and the number is not to be taken as an indication of exclusivity of merit. They were chosen, first of all, because each has published a sufficiently large body of work to make sense of an attempt to trace their growth and continuing contribution. This has meant leaving out many noteworthy dramatists (John Herbert, Beverley Simons, Lister Sinclair, for example) whose published works include only one or two plays, and those whose works are available only in manuscript or typescript. The lack of published English translations of most of our French-language authors, moreover, has led to the omission of some of the most exciting Canadian dramatists now at work; it is to be hoped that translations of the plays of Marcel Dubé, Jacques Languirand, Michel Tremblay and others will soon become more widely procurable.[1] Perhaps we shall soon, also, see more essays on the work of earlier playwrights, and on the work of such promising newcomers as David Freeman, David French and Roch Carrier. Within the limited space available, however, our four authors do reflect various regions, styles and attitudes.

I have used every opportunity to place each of our dramatists within the context of the development of the theatre as a whole in Canada, since that necessary background of knowledge is also often missing. The lack is hardly surprising; we have as yet no full history of English-language theatre in Canada, while Jean Béraud's excellent *Three Hundred and Twenty Years of Theatre in French Canada* has not yet been translated into English. In fact one of the most serious difficulties in introducing the whole subject of theatre in Canada is that we must study our theatrical history from U.S. or British texts which

---

[1] As we go to press, additional English translations of Canadian plays in French have been announced. (See p. 88)

either ignore its existence, or, like the *Oxford Companion to the Theatre,* imagine it recently sprang from nowhere.

The substantial excerpts which follow each essay— amounting to a complete scene from one of the author's three-act plays—are designed to demonstrate the claims and comments advanced in each essay. They should, of course, be used for this purpose, and not as a substitute for reading the entire play. In classes, they will (it is hoped) whet the student's appetite for further reading, and elicit, by being read aloud, some discussion about the author's success in achieving what he set out to do. Above all, these scenes afford—in a mode impossible for any commentary—a glimpse of the writer's way with character and dialogue, and of his theatrical style.

In an Endnote will be found some suggestions for further enquiry and research. Here necessity can be turned into a virtue: the very lack of secondary research materials provides an exciting opportunity for primary research. Wherever the reader is located, *some* additional sources are at hand—newspaper files, journals, libraries, onetime performers or theatregoers, collections of old programs, perhaps an old "Opera House"—and other sources may be found through trips, inter-library loans, and the like. If the few titles listed succeed in arousing interest in the writers and their works, then perhaps further reading and theatre-going will follow naturally.

1 Background

The excuse most often given for the shortage of playwrights of note in Canada is that it is a young country, from which too much should not be expected too soon. This is not only a feeble excuse, it is no excuse at all: Montreal is far older as a metropolis than New York, and Toronto than Los Angeles. There are valid explanations for our sins of omission; they relate to the whole history of the country, however, and reach far beyond the scope of this little book. But we must recognize several of them here, even if only to alert the reader for echoes of them in what follows.

To begin with, the playwright must have a theatre. Theatre is to a large extent dependent on language, and in Canada we have two large language groups. The main French-speaking province, Quebec, sits between the eastern provinces on the one hand, and the central and western provinces on the other. There are natural barriers even between Ontario and the Prairie Provinces, and between them and British Columbia. This inevitable fragmentation has had a profound effect on our theatre—for theatres must either stay in one very large central place to which audiences may come, or travel to seek them out. In the nineteenth century this meant that different troupes (often based in the United States) played an "eastern," "central," "western" or "Pacific" circuit; in the twentieth century it meant, first, disastrously expensive tours across Canada, and an attempt to establish regional theatres. These uneconomic enterprises were doomed by the simultaneous onslaught of the "talkies" and the depression of the nineteen-thirties. The professional theatre, which had been active for a century or more (except in Quebec, where it was for long repressed by the Church), left the field to the amateurs—who could far more economically serve each of the still divided regions.

Such professional groups as managed to exist *in* Canada in the late nineteenth and early twentieth centuries did on occasion present plays by Canadian authors. But generally, like the most ambitious of our actors, promising dramatists traded in their nationality for one more self-confident, and became, so far as their public were concerned, American or British or French. These were the days when Julia Arthur, Clara Morris and later Maude Adams, Margaret Anglin and Walter Huston left Ontario to become Broadway stars, and Bea Lillie and Raymond Massey set out to conquer London; when Mack Sennett (from Quebec), the Warner Brothers and Louis B. Mayer (from New Brunswick), Mary Pickford and Marie Dressler (from Ontario) went south to Hollywood to help shape forever the new art-industry of film. Our dramatists were also busy toiling for other mills: Montreal's W. A. Tremayne wrote turn-of-the-century melodramas for the great U.S. stars, and Hamilton's Charles Bell wrote some of the raciest of nineteen-twenties Broadway farces. But even after the watershed of 1930, when Canadians wrote such international successes as *Whiteoaks* (Mazo de la Roche), *Teach Me How to Cry* (Patricia Joudry) or the more recent *Fortune and Men's Eyes* (John Herbert), the productions abroad showed few marks of their birthplace: in setting and accent they became indistinguishable from British and American plays. Canadians did not even know each other: how could the world be expected to recognize them? And what would be the point of emphasizing any unidentifiable differences? The theatre as a mirror of their society hardly existed for Canadians; for others it showed nothing but a blank face.

It should come as no surprise, then, that it was radio—which could link the nation in a way beyond the resources of the living theatre—which provided us with our first national dramatic expression. Commencing in 1941, the *Stage* series of the Canadian Broadcasting Corporation, under the brilliant producer-director Andrew Allan, provided Canadian dramatists, actors and composers with their first real chance to be themselves, to speak in their own accents about things of direct concern to themselves—and to their audience. A similar movement in radio was started in Quebec. And the Second World War brought a growing awareness—if not of a national identity, at least of the lack of one, of a need to *belong somewhere* instead of being *from* nowhere in particular. Canadians began to speak of coming "home," and at long last they didn't mean the country they or their forebears had left to come to Canada.

But the long history of being either Nobody or Someone Else had taken its toll: as the following essays and excerpts show, when the living theatre finally found its own rebirth, in both English and French Canada, commencing in the late 1940s, our writers of all kinds—east and west, comedians, tragedians, satirists, old guard and avant-garde alike—seemed to be gripped by one root theme. As Northrop Frye puts it in his remarkable essay *The Bush Garden:*

> It seems to me that Canadian sensibility has been profoundly disturbed, not so much by our famous problem of identity, important as that is, as by a series of paradoxes in what confronts that identity. It is less perplexed by the question "Who am I?" than by some such riddle as "Where is here?"

James Reaney might be speaking for most Canadian playwrights and their works when he heads one section of his play *Colours in the Dark* with the explanation: "This sequence is about beginning to wonder where you've come from; then beginning to wonder where you're going." The questions of knowing who one is and where one belongs depend, eventually, on establishing contact with some sort of frame of reference; we may be sending out radar signals like mad, but unless and until they are bounced back we cannot plot our position.

Literature and the visual and performing arts are the conventional means by which a society reflects and defines itself, and by which the individuals in that society can place themselves. The Canadian playwright has therefore found himself acting as both mirror and image: in reflecting his own society he cannot avoid reflecting both his and its endeavour to find a focus. His plays are both *about* the search for a self and a place, and a demonstration of that search.

Whether that search is of any consequence to others may be an open question, but it is certainly of immense importance to us. And the very process of attempting to define ourselves, in fact, provides at least some of the reference-points we need to discover "Where is here? " On the way home, there have been others only too eager to praise or damn the towns and countryside we pass through; my aim has been, rather, to provide a road-map for the reader, and to suggest interesting signs and aspects to watch for in the work of our playwrights. We have a long way to go—but this book is dedicated to the proposition that we are demonstrably getting there.

2 Robertson Davies

In his introduction to Robertson Davies' first published collection of plays (all short) in 1949, Tyrone Guthrie wrote:

> It is typical of this phase of Canadian development that Robertson Davies should have "finished" his education abroad . . . By the time he had left "Finishing School" in Oxford and London, he was equipped to begin the education of a Canadian citizen and man of letters, equipped to be one of the pioneers of the still imaginary Canadian Theatre.

Four years later, with the advent of the Guthrie-guided Stratford Festival in Ontario, and the launching of the Théâtre du Nouveau Monde in Quebec, the Canadian Theatre was a reality. Canadian playwrights, however, were conspicuous by their absence at the attendant celebrations—it being the current joke that the country's outstanding dramatists were two expatriates named Shakespeare and Molière. In 1949 it would have taken a closer knowledge of the local scene than the British Guthrie then possessed to foresee a break in the clouds for native playwrights; but in the previous year there had been two auspicious omens. In Montreal Gratien Gélinas had created our first home-grown hit with his *Tit-Coq,* and in Toronto the New Play Society's production of Morley Callaghan's *To Tell the Truth* had moved from its tiny Museum Theatre to become the first all-Canadian show ever to play in the forty-three-year-old Royal Alexandra—until then a local showcase for foreign companies.

But we are getting ahead of our story. Davies had returned to Canada in 1940, nine years before his first plays were published, to find theatre little changed since his youth. He was born in 1913 of Welsh and Scots parentage, a particularly flammable Celtic mixture. Well-to-do thanks to his father's industriousness, he attended Upper Canada College and early showed talent as an actor in addition to excellence as a scholar—another highly combustible combination, although by no means as rare as is often believed. He pursued these aptitudes at Oxford, after a few years at Queen's University in Ontario, and his thesis on *Shakespeare's Boy Actors* became a distinguished book. After a brief whirl in the professional theatre at London's Old Vic, he ostensibly gave up acting and returned home to become a journalist and, he hoped, a playwright. (I say "ostensibly" because it is my view, as we shall see, that he never gave it up at all.)

His welcome was less than enthusiastic. Not long afterwards, under his journalistic alias Samuel Marchbanks, he wrote a grimly sardonic letter on the subject to a fictitious correspondent.

Dear Mr. Fishorn:

You want to be a Canadian playwright, and ask me for advice as to how to set about it. Well, Fishorn, the first thing you had better acquaint yourself with is the physical conditions of the Canadian theatre. Every great drama, as you know, has been shaped by its playhouse . . .

Now what is the Canadian playhouse? Nine times out of ten, Fishorn, it is a school hall, smelling of chalk and kids, and decorated in the Early Concrete style. The stage is a small raised room at one end. And I mean room. If you step into the wings suddenly you will fracture your nose against the wall. There is no place for storing scenery, no place for the actors to dress, and the lighting is designed to warm the stage but not to illuminate it.

Write your plays, then, for such a stage . . . Place as many scenes as you can in cellars and kindred spots. And don't have more than three characters on the stage at one time, or the weakest of them is sure to be nudged into the audience.

Farewell, and good luck to you.

The exaggeration was only slight; although there were, in most larger cities and towns, splendid theatres for visiting companies from other countries, the only theatre which might be persuaded to put on plays by new and unknown authors was the ardent but fumbling "Little Theatre." Only our radio drama was then professionally skilful—and Marchbanks/Davies wanted the real stuff: live theatre. So he wrote, at first, for the amateurs.

The five one-act plays in the earliest collection were all comedies, but different enough to show at once his wide range of interest and style. *Eros at Breakfast* is a fantasy laid in the stomach of a young man falling in love, with an appropriate conflict between the Solar Plexus, the Brain, the Heart, the Liver and other deeply affected organs; Davies, like G. B. Shaw, relished backing each side of the debate in its turn. *The Voice of the People* is a naturalistic domestic pleasantry with an uncanny similitude to lower-middle-class family life in an Ontario small town, based on an incident dear to a journalist's heart: a letter-to-the-editor. *Hope Deferred* is a dramatization of an actual event in Canadian history, showing Frontenac as an early champion of the arts in a colonial society (note the title). *Overlaid* is a droll parable about an old man still full of life, at odds with a daughter-in-law who suffers from a familiar Canadian complaint: Paralyzing Puritanitis. *At the Gates of the Righteous* is a farcical send-up of "our hallowed pioneer past," in which a young rebel learns that lawlessness is not much fun without the law. The form and focus of each is different; but in common they show a rare ability to enter into a wide variety of characters, a remarkable ear for the speech of many places and social levels, an ebullient sense of humour, disrespect for sacred cows and a sophisticate's abhorrence of everything and everyone dull. It will be noticed that the first two are qualities one would expect from an actor—and the second is a knack one might expect from a *Canadian* actor especially, for we have had to learn to perform in every dialect of English but our own. The others almost constitute a definition of a literary humourist.

Now curiously—or so some may think—humour, and especially satirical humour, is a long-standing tradition in Canadian arts and letters. From "Sam Slick" through Stephen Leacock to today's topical Revues, mocking our own insignificance has been our handiest safety-valve, and thumbing our noses at our betters has been one way of living with the cultivated Europeans and the rich Americans. Robertson Davies is squarely in this tradition. But to play the funny side of everything one must, he warns us, be aware of the flip-side as well:

> What little I know of humour suggests that it is not something which a man possesses, but rather something which possesses him; it is constantly in operation, it has a dark as well as a light aspect, and its function is by no means that of keeping its possessor in fits of chuckles.

Possessed by humour, then, Davies has poured out over the years a stream of books, eighteen so far—plays, novels, criticism, essays, even an almanac—and all the while holding full-time jobs, first as editor and later as university professor (which he still is). There is nothing so cheerless as analysing humour (even Leacock was boring when he tried it), but it is important to get a line on what Davies finds funny about *us*—of all people.

The first of his six (so far) full-length plays was *Fortune, My Foe*, written and produced in 1949. This was the time, you will remember, when the professional theatre was rising again, and beginning to look for Canadian plays. Davies quickly obliged (too quickly, he now feels), picking up a theme introduced in *Hope Deferred* and *Overlaid*: the lot of the artist and the intellectual in Canada, "overlaid by a stultifying home atmosphere and cultural malnutrition." It may not sound like it, but in his own way he was tackling the root questions of home, family and identity as they were posed by the times.

Nicholas Hayward, a brilliant young professor of English, has been offered a lucrative post in the United States. Wanting to satisfy his rich and discontented girl-friend Vanessa, he is talking himself into accepting it against the advice of his mentor, old Professor Rowlands. Rowlands, educated in England, is embittered by the lacklustre Canadian treadmill, but thinks Nicholas will ruin himself as a scholar if he goes south "for money." They meet in the old hangar on the outskirts of town, which the practical "Chilly" Steele has set up as a restaurant and sometime speak-easy, and where he is sheltering a jobless European refugee. Franz Szabo is the latest of a long line of puppeteers, and fancies that one day he will recreate their great art here. A friendly newspaper editor introduces some

12

prospective clients: a woman who wants to use puppets for political propaganda plays, and two zealots from the local department of education. Nicholas and Vanessa help Szabo with a hastily rigged presentation of *Don Quixote*, which shocks and stumps the auditioners. But Szabo will not compromise his art; he sees Canada as a land of opportunity precisely because it needs him. With this example, Nicholas decides to stay, and parts from Vanessa.

A straightforward story, you might think, and a typical Canadian situation—caught between the spiritual superiority of Europe and the material superiority of the United States. But I have left out the cream of the jest: Davies introduces, as a kind of disgraceful Greek chorus to these lofty goings-on, an old wino who hangs about showing to any soft touch the collection of "artistic" postcards from which he used to make his living. Buckety Murphy has Art and Sensuality all hilariously mixed up; but could it be the old bum is onto something? Is art not more likely to arise from sheer animal spirits than from the rule-books of conventional minds? Murphy, as well as Rowlands, is a victim of "this raw, frost-bitten country" and "its raw, frost-bitten people." Who can call it home? —only idealistic newcomers such as Franz Szabo, or those with "hope deferred," such as Nicholas:

> Everybody says Canada is a hard country to govern, but nobody mentions that for some people it is also a hard country to live in. Still, if we all run away, it will never be any better. So let the geniuses of easy virtue go southward; I know what they feel too well to blame them. But for some of us there is no choice; let Canada do what she will with us, we must stay.

If Nicholas speaks for author Davies, so does Buckety Murphy. That is to say, Davies is no intellectual snob poking fun at the illiterate, but a champion of the affirmative against the negative. His targets are not the know-nothings but the do-nothings, the smug, faint-hearted mediocrities who ride on the coat-tails of civilization but contribute nothing, and who spend their time telling others "Thou shalt not" or "Thou canst not." Among the things Davies had been assured Canadians could not do was to write plays—especially about Canadians, because they are so bland. He turned the tables by shamelessly putting his far-from-bland self on display: he wrote about himself (skilfully disguising parts of himself as Solar Plexus, Brain, Heart, Liver, etc.), casting himself in all the roles, and making us laugh at and with ourselves. He was, in fact, acting out our identity.

He continued to do this in his next play, *At My Heart's Core* (1950), an historical work set in the rebellious Upper Canada of 1837. Two famous literary ladies, the English-born Susanna Moodie and her sister Mrs. Traill, are visiting the neighbouring home of the Honourable Thomas Stewart, who has gone off to York on business. The Irish Mrs. Stewart and her guests are being besieged by the disreputable Phelim Brady, whose fiancée and infant daughter are being protected within. Another visitor arrives, a strange Anglo-Irishman named Cantwell, who is disenchanted with Canada and plans to return to Britain. Staying to protect them against the drunken Brady, Cantwell tempts each of the women in turn—not with love, but with their own discontent: "New countries mean not only hopes fulfilled but hopes relinquished." Stewart returns, settles Brady's domestic problems, sends Cantwell on his superior way, and gives promise to the ladies of a better life to come.

Once again, each of the characters has something of Davies in him or her. But his sympathies obviously lie less with the smooth intellectual Cantwell, who is right but all negative, than with the old reprobate Phelim, who is all wrong but affirmative: "And isn't a poet and story-teller miles above and beyond them common fellows is diggin' the ground and pullin' out stumps?" But even Phelim has to admit "We're the songbirds that aren't wanted in this bitter land, where the industrious robins and the political crows get fat, and they with not a tuneful chirp among the lot of 'em! " But the ladies, like Nicholas in *Fortune, My Foe,* are determined to stay and change things.

Another comedy, *Hunting Stuart*, brings up-to-date the conflict of loyalties between Old Country and new country, while in *A Jig for the Gypsy* (1954), Robertson Davies demonstrates that conflict in himself by writing an historical play set in nineteenth-century Wales. But we must note a new dark thread in these—in fact its first traces are evident in the sinister

Cantwell in *At My Heart's Core*: the idea of temptation, which was naturalistically handled in *Fortune, My Foe*, is now being personified. Occult rituals begin to appear in the plays—the wooing of gods or devils—as if our author, tiring of playing devil's advocate with his characters, now wanted supernatural help. His novel *Tempest-Tost*, superficially an hilarious jape about an amateur production of Shakespeare's *The Tempest*, is in fact a carefully worked-out mythical parallel to that magical play. A similar pattern of good and evil spirits is observable in his second and third novels, *Leaven of Malice* and *A Mixture of Frailities*, and moves right into the foreground of his more recent novels, *Fifth Business* and *The Manticore*. His play *General Confession* is about Casanova, an expert in temptation both worldly and otherworldly.

Like Oscar Wilde, Davies sees life as far too important to be taken seriously. Canadians take themselves very seriously indeed, perhaps because they feel themselves to be unimportant. It would seem as if Robertson Davies, trying to make them think better of themselves, at some point decided the Devil himself could do a better job than R. Davies acting the Devil—if only he could invoke the Prince of Darkness to play Davies. (Davies, of course, has not stopped acting just because he has summoned the Devil; he is, after all, still the magician.) He became fascinated with the way in which an evil deed often stirs us to good, while good intentions lead us to Hell. Could it be that what this country needed was a stiff dose of wickedness? That is the idea behind *Leaven of Malice*, which he later turned into the play *Love and Libel* (1960).

The evil deed concerned is (like the tiny cake of yeast which later leavens) a small act of malice. An engagement notice is inserted in the newspaper of Davies' customary Ontario town (usually a thinly-disguised Kingston) which links two young people who do not like each other, Solly Bridgetower and Pearl Vambrace. *His* clinging mother thinks it is intended to embarrass her, and *her* dominating father thinks it is meant to humiliate him. No one knows the author of the hoax, but everyone suspects everyone else, and all become entangled in the consequences—the newspaper editor, the minister, the pillars of church and society, a lawyer, a psychologist. Eventually, the false notice is the means of bringing Solly and Pearl to leave their respective overpowering parents and to fall in love. As usual, there is the counterpoint provided by a social outcast, in this case the bohemian choir leader Humphrey Cobbler, whose artistic talents are not appreciated.

The old themes are all here, with a stronger emphasis on family relationships and the attempt of the young to find an identity of their own. But—risky as it is to pin philosophies on a man who keeps changing hats—the main theme seems to be that of temptation. You can only grow up, Davies seems to be saying, when you have been tempted by the Devil, faced up to him, and thus know yourself and where you are going. To achieve this rebirth you require evil as well as good. And that is the way in which Canadians will discover themselves.

This resolution of his own character, of the various elements within himself, came to Robertson Davies only after he had acted out all those elements in a wide variety of dramatic forms. The clearest statement of his own transformation is contained in one of the two Masques he wrote for the boys of Upper Canada College, *A Masque of Aesop* (1952), in which the fabulist is judged by the god Apollo (the sun, with its life-giving *and* life-destroying power):

> I rebuke you for the arrogance of your wisdom; perfect wisdom is an attribute of the gods alone . . . The greatest teacher is he who has passed through scorn of mankind, to love of mankind.

It is easy to see in Davies' development the traditional struggle between Romantic and Classical impulses (one all heart, the other all brain); in fact he calls himself a Romantic while many of his critics consider him a Classicist—which should alert us to the likelihood that this is an ongoing tension which has *not* been resolved. One can also see in his works a tension between the two Celtic traditions, Welsh and Scottish: mysticism versus rationalism. But the one tension which Davies *has* resolved, it seems to me, is that between the Actor and the Intellectual. He has found a way, by putting the intellect at the service of the actor in him (instead of vice versa, as he began), of being himself. He has confronted his own Demon and found out who he is.

Although most foreign critics naturally miss it, part of the point of the teacher Dunstan Ramsey in Davies' highly successful novel *Fifth Business* is that *like most Canadians* he is doomed to play only a variety of supporting roles. In his youth this bothered him:

> I seemed to be the only person I knew without a plan that would put the world on its feet and wipe the tear from every eye. No wonder I felt like a stranger in my own land.

But Ramsey meets the Devil and tweaks his (in this case her) nose, and comes to terms with himself. Even he, like the amoral puppet Punch in *A Masque of Mr. Punch*, has the power within him—it does not lie outside—to be his own Unregenerate Man. An actor is "one who does" as well as "one who represents"; and in the act of representing his fellow-countrymen Davies has already changed our image of ourselves. We cannot be all that dull because he is never dull about us. And he is one of us.

EXTRACT FROM *FORTUNE, MY FOE*
BY ROBERTSON DAVIES

Nicholas Hayward, a young professor, meets his friend, the older Professor Idris Rowlands, at "Chilly" Steele's "equivocal establishment" by the river. (Steele runs a sort of restaurant where he provides for his friends the drinks the law did not, at that time, allow them. He is sheltering a European refugee, Franz Szabo, a puppeteeer who is not yet a legal immigrant.) Nicholas has announced his intention of furthering his academic career in the United States—against which Rowlands has been arguing.

NICHOLAS:
I'm sorry if I was nagging at you, Idris. I've been edgy for a day or two. Beginning of an academic year, I suppose.

A scene from Act One of Fortune My Foe. *From left to right: Frank Peddie as "Buckety" Murphy, Barry Morse as Idris Rowlands, Lloyd Bochner as Nicholas, Murray Westgate as Ed Weir.*

ROWLANDS:

No. You find fault with me because you are discontented with yourself. And you are discontented with yourself because of what you are doing there. You are not the man, Nicholas, to leave Canada for money.

NICHOLAS:

Damn it all, why does everybody talk as though it were criminal for a scholar to want money? And what is sacred about the Canadian scale of payment for academic services? Is it disgraceful to want to make a name, to—to seek some recognition for whatever talents one may have?

ROWLANDS:

Isn't it an odd thing to fight for a country, only to leave it for another?

NICHOLAS:

I didn't fight for a country. Some men did, but I did not. I fought for an ideal, and that ideal is more honoured in the States than it is here.

ROWLANDS:

The ideal of money, perhaps?

NICHOLAS:

No, and you know that is not true. It is an ideal of civilization, an ideal in which a high standard of living means something more than merely a high standard of eating—

ROWLANDS:

And you expect to find that in the States? The Americans are to the civilization of our day what the Romans were to the civilization of the ancient world; they are its middle-men, its popularizers, not its creaters.

NICHOLAS:

Yes, but behind all the commercialism and vulgarity there is a promise, and there is no promise here, as yet, for men like me. I am not patient! But I am not unreasonable! I can live on a promise, but in a country where the questions that I ask meet only with blank incomprehension, and the yearnings that I feel find no understanding I know that I must go mad, or I must strangle my soul with my own hands, or I must get out and try my luck in a country which has some use for me!

ROWLANDS:
You have a place here.

NICHOLAS:
Despised because I do not teach anything useful. Despised because I want things from life which nobody else seems to miss. Despised because my abilities command so little money—

ROWLANDS:
Money! Back to it again.

Money is also a problem for Franz Szabo, who badly needs a livelihood. Their mutual friend Ed Weir, the editor of the local newspaper, suggests that Szabo might get a job doing or teaching puppetry in the schools, and proposes bringing along some educationists to see his work. It is Szabo's determination to stay in Canada and fight, rather than to run away again, which eventually changes Nicholas' mind. This scene, in Act II, is the play's turning point. (Nicholas sits at one table with his fiancée, Vanessa, and the "propagandist" Ursula)

At this point WEIR returns with ORVILLE TAPSCOTT, an exuberant, busy man, and MRS. E. C. PHILPOTT, who, as a keen advocate of all arts and crafts, wears a great many ornaments in tortured metal and outraged leather; even her spectacles have a hand-made look. Both are a-twitter at finding themselves in CHILLY'S den.

TAPSCOTT:
Well, I must say this doesn't look too bad. I was in a lot tougher looking joints than this when I was school-inspecting up in the north.

MATTIE:
I suppose the crowd doesn't begin to come till late.

20

WEIR:
There is never a crowd here, Mrs. Philpott.

CHILLY:
Good evening, Mr. Weir. I see you've brought a couple of friends. Respectable people, I hope?

WEIR:
Yes, Chilly, I'll be their guarantee.

CHILLY:
That's good enough. No offence, folks, but a man can't be too careful who comes into his place nowadays. Some awful rowdies around.

TAPSCOTT:
(*heartily*) You don't think we look like rowdies, I hope?

CHILLY:
A fellow never knows. It was your friend who kind of worried me. So much jewellery. Kind of arouses suspicions.

MATTIE:
But that's craft jewellery. I make it myself.

CHILLY:
Well, just so long as you come by it respectably.

MATTIE:
Well really! I think I'm pretty well known in this town.

CHILLY:
I don't care about that just so long as you don't start anything here. Keep your voice down and go home with the fellow you came with. That's all I ask, and it's little enough.

TAPSCOTT:
You're all wrong. This is Mrs. E. C. Philpott, president of the Ladies Craft Culture Club, Women's Convenor of the Hobby Lobby, and chairwoman of the crafts sub-committee of the local Recreation Commission. You've heard of Mattie Philpott?

21

CHILLY:

Nope.

TAPSCOTT:

I'm Tapscott. Never heard of me, either, I suppose.

CHILLY:

Nope.

TAPSCOTT:

Well, it's refreshing to meet with such ignorance. I guess you live completely outside the recreation field.

CHILLY:

Depends what you mean. Some people consider this the centre of the recreation field.

MATTIE:

Recreation means "re-creation." What you sell here doesn't create: it destroys.

NICHOLAS:

May I have another cup of this excellent coffee, Chilly?

CHILLY:

Right away.

NICHOLAS:

And could I have an egg sandwich, as well? Not too heavy on the condiments, if you please. Good evening, Mrs. Philpott; didn't we meet at the Crystal Craft exhibition last spring?

MATTIE:

Why, Mr Hayward! I didn't expect to meet you here.

NICHOLAS:

To tell you the truth, I didn't expect to meet you here, either. You are so busy with your recreation activities that I don't suppose you have much time for enjoyment. But I come here often to look across the water at the city, and enjoy a cup of Chilly's wonderful coffee. May I offer you a cup?

MATTIE:
Well, to tell you the truth, I had three cups at supper.

NICHOLAS:
A cold fruit juice, then. No no, you mustn't refuse me. And you too, Mr. Tapscott. We haven't met, but I have heard many people speak of you.

TAPSCOTT:
Thanks. Very kind, I'm sure.

NICHOLAS:
Chilly, two delicious, vitamin-packed juices. A hop in every drop. What about you, Ned?

WEIR:
Coffee.

NICHOLAS:
You seem pensive. What's the matter?

WEIR:
(*drawing him aside*) Don't kid these people, Nick. They may be able to help Szabo.

NICHOLAS:
Fantastic! How?

WEIR:
Give me a chance.

CHILLY has brought fruit drinks for TAPSCOTT and MRS. PHILPOTT; they are in tall glasses, iced and with tall sprigs of mint in them; they do not look innocent. Later he brings coffee for NICHOLAS and WEIR.

NICHOLAS:
I understand that you are here on business, so I shall return to my table. But I hope that before you go you will be able to

meet my friends. Unless you intend to stay very late, of course. (*He goes back to VANESSA and URSULA.*)

TAPSCOTT:
Say, this is certainly good juice! Do you sell much of it?

CHILLY:
Gallons, and gallons, and gallons.

TAPSCOTT:
Would you consider selling me the formula? I'd like to put this into the juice bars of every regional recreation centre in the city. This is just what the teenager wants. A juice with a tang!

MATTIE:
You certainly fix it up nicely. It almost looks wicked. Dainty serving certainly makes a big difference.

CHILLY:
Thanks. That's the first time anyone ever called me dainty.

WEIR:
Is Franz around, Chilly?

CHILLY:
In the kitchen. *(Shouts)* Franz!

SZABO:
(outside) Yes! *(He comes in, still carrying his bit of carving.)*

WEIR:
This is Franz Szabo. I've told you about him. Franz, Mrs. Philpott and Mr. Tapscott are interested in your work and I want to see if you can be of use to each other.

SZABO:
Oh yes. It is very kind of you to come.

MATTIE:
I still don't understand why you couldn't meet us at the Y.W.C.A.

WEIR:

That's a long story. The point is have you any use for a first-class puppet man, and can you help Franz to get on his feet in Canada?

TAPSCOTT:

Well, let's be perfectly frank. Let's get right down to work and lay our cards on the table face upwards. Puppets are nothing new here.

SZABO:

No. They are not very new anywhere.

TAPSCOTT:

Puppets have had a place in the recreational field for years. In fact, at least six puppet groups have been formed right here in our own city. How are they making out, Mrs. Philpott?

MATTIE:

Well, just at present there isn't much activity; in fact, I think we've pretty well exhausted the puppet. But then, summer is barely over, and we stress outdoor activities in the fine weather. Puppets are only practical in schools, you see.

SZABO:

Oh? Why?

TAPSCOTT:

Well, puppetry comes under the head of what we call tot-to-teen activities. Simple handicrafts to encourage manual dexterity. After fourteen we figure that the teenager is adjusting to sex and society and he needs group-training and vigorous outdoor sports.

SZABO:

But I do not understand. Puppetry is not at all simple. How far did your groups go with their work?

MATTIE:

Oh, a complete course. Hand puppets—Punch and Judy, you know—then marionettes—the string figures, you understand—and Javanese shadow puppets. It was a very thorough program. Each child had to make at least one puppet.

SZABO:

But who taught all this?

MATTIE:

Miss McConkey of the Collegiate staff; she did a six weeks' summer course in it last year at the College of Education.

SZABO:

But Madame, how—? Six weeks?

MATTIE:

She was really wonderful. She simplified what she had learned for the children, of course. For instance, all the puppets were dressed in long skirts, so that they didn't need any legs, you see. Children find it very hard to make a puppet walk. And the heads were really doll's heads that she bought in the five-and-ten, to get around all the trouble of modelling. You see, Mr. Szabo, it's no use expecting children to stick to anything that seems difficult. Our recreational courses are worked out on the most modern methods of teaching, and we know that the minute a problem is created, interest wanes.

SZABO:

But surely, in games—

TAPSCOTT:

Oh, a game is an entirely different proposition.

SZABO:

I should say so. Puppets are a very serious matter. I am sure that Miss—Miss what-you-said, is a very charming lady, but in six weeks she could not even get the feel of a single puppet, not to speak of Javanese puppets, and all the puppets in the world. Indeed—I must be frank—women do not make puppet masters. The women of my family made costumes and played the music, but the puppets were handled by the men.

TAPSCOTT:

Oh, you'll find it very different here. Puppetry is a girl's project—the sub-teen girl. And scientific teaching speeds up the course.

26

SZABO:

Ach, Gott! And do you want me to teach these little girls to play with dolls that have no legs?

TAPSCOTT:

No, no; Miss McConkey has done all that. As a matter of cold fact, the puppet needs a shot in the arm here; as a project the puppet has fallen flat. We want to put the puppet on its feet from a scientific recreational point of view.

SZABO:

How can a puppet be on its feet when it has no feet?

TAPSCOTT:

Well, what we feel is this. The puppet is a flop as a manual-development project, but there is still a place for the puppet in the social instructional field.

MATTIE:

Yes, we feel that the puppet has a great future in the tot-lot.

SZABO:

Please, what is it, a lot-tot?

MATTIE:

Tot-lot. It's just what it says—a lot full of tots.

WEIR:

Franz, a lot is a piece of open ground, and a tot is a child.

MATTIE:

Not just any child; recreationally speaking, the tot is the three-to-eight age group.

TAPSCOTT:

And morons from three to sixteen.

MATTIE:

Yes, of course. We have to include morons. Now what do you want to get across to the tot?

SZABO:

God knows.

MATTIE:

Socially acceptable behaviour, of course. Now the question is: how?

SZABO:

Ach so; how?

TAPSCOTT:

(merrily pretending to blow a trumpet) Ta-ta-ta-ta! Enter the puppet!

MATTIE:

This is Orville's idea, and it appears to me to be one of the greatest strokes of genius in organized recreation!

TAPSCOTT:

Here you are, an experienced hand with puppets. You whip up a dozen little plays, based on pamphlets we can give you, and you tour the tot-lots. You set up your little show and you do a ten-minute play, let's say, about a kid who doesn't eat his cereal for breakfast. What happens? He gets sick, and a big dragon called Malnutrition comes to him and says, "Lookit, you've got to eat your cereal." So he does, and when the play ends, he's happy.

MATTIE:

It helps to assimilate the child to the group, you see. It will revolutionize social training in the tot-lot.

TAPSCOTT:

Or take teeth. Kid won't clean his teeth. He goes to bed and dreams he's living in a big white castle that is falling down. Everywhere he goes, things fall apart. Then he discovers he's living in a decayed tooth. He wakes up and says: "I'll always clean my teeth after this. Kids, clean your teeth night and morning and remove particles from between your teeth with dental floss." Curtain.

SZABO:

Mr. Tapscott, I—I don't know what to say.

TAPSCOTT:
Oh I understand. This is a big idea and it has to be dealt with in a big way. Mind you, I'm not talking officially now. I'm not even talking on committee level, not to mention executive level. But if you can fix up a few shows, we'll put them on at the inter-regional recreational directors' conference next month, and if they don't throw the meeting into an uproar, well, my name's not Orville Tapscott, that's all.

MATTIE:
I just can't see it failing, Orville.

TAPSCOTT:
Well, Mattie, not everybody in the recreational field has your vision. But mark my words, Szabo, if it goes over, there's no limit to what can follow. Why, the whole audio-visual field opens before us!

SZABO:
The—?

TAPSCOTT:
Audio-visuals. You know, talking pictures. Or didn't they have them in Europe when you left?

SZABO:
Yes, but how can you mix marionettes and talking pictures?

TAPSCOTT:
Easily. We film the shows, and exhibit them in schools. Audio-visuals are the coming thing in education. They reduce pupil-resistance by cutting down pupil-effort to the barest minimum. But that's all to come. First we have to win the battle of the tot-lot.

MATTIE:
You know, Orville, it's masterly. The more you talk about it, the better it sounds.

TAPSCOTT:
Thanks, Mat. You know how I feel about your support on this thing. And I've always said that there isn't another woman in

the recreational field with your breadth. Well, there's the plan, Szabo. Now let's just kick it around till something comes out of it.

SZABO:

Mr. Tapscott, may I say something now?

TAPSCOTT:

Go ahead.

SZABO:

This plan; it will not do.

TAPSCOTT:

Now just a minute. Let's get this straight. The plan is all right. Maybe you won't do. Maybe you haven't the vision. But the plan is all right.

SZABO:

No, Mr. Tapscott, the plan is not all right. It is all wrong. It is—what do you say? —cheap and nasty. You say that I should kick it around. Very well, now I shall kick—

TAPSCOTT:

Now just a minute. I have had long experience in the recreational field—

SZABO:

But I have had longer experience of puppets. I have my own, and my father's, and my grandfather's, back to the time of Shakespeare. I did not learn what I know in six weeks from some other ignoramus. A puppet is a little jointed figure, and I am the puppet master. Yes? But also the puppet is a man, and I am the god who gives him life and a soul—a part of my own soul. I make him so carefully, piece by piece, that I know him better than I know my own body: I do not make him from cheap dolls with no legs. And when I know him, and make him walk and move his arms and dance I concentrate so hard on him that he is more truly alive than I am myself. He is myself. Now, Mr. Tapscott, tell me: do I use all my skill and inherited tradition and knowledge to make little children eat nasty food or rub their teeth with brushes? Are fifteen generations of puppet

30

masters to end with a harlot of a dirty dog who uses his art to tell nonsense? Don't speak! I know this is the new world and the atomic age, but I know that what has taken three hundred years to make does not lose its value in a few weeks. You are wrong, Mr. Tapscott, and if your nonsense is what your country believes, it is time your country got some sense!

NICHOLAS:

Hear hear!

3 Gratien Gélinas

On November 7, 1873, Archbishop Taschereau of Quebec ordered a letter to be read from the pulpit of every church in his see, banning Catholics from attending the theatres—"those dens of all the vices." His edict was splendidly successful among those concerned with their social status in this world and the next, but only persuaded less righteous folk that the theatre must be more fun than ever. The result was that humble sinners by the thousands ignored the ban and packed the performances of operetta and vaudeville troupes from the United States and France, while the theatre as a serious native art form went "under the snows" for seventy years. What survived was only the literary study of classical drama in the schools and seminaries.

Ironically, it was under the aegis of the same Roman Catholic Church that a renascence in theatre occurred in the province at about the time of World War II. A quiet revolution was afoot: in Canada generally, and in Quebec in particular, a new self-awareness was rising, a confidence that to be different did not mean to be second-rate. In 1938, Father Emile Legault of the Congrégation de Sainte-Croix formed a troupe of amateurs, Les Compagnons de Saint-Laurent, to present religious plays. Realizing the larger need of an audience starved for French-language theatre, he soon moved into the production of secular classics by Molière and Racine, and even into modern plays by Cocteau, Anouilh and Giraudoux. His young company—from which came such later luminaries of the Canadian theatre as Jean Gascon and Jean-Louis Roux, and their Théâtre du Nouveau Monde—established a remarkable standard of acting, visual design, and technical skill. Demanding and vigorous as its training was, however, the company's stamp was still fundamentally that of a transplanted French classical theatre, not unlike the similar fashion in English-speaking Canada for anglicized Shakespeare. It was, that is to say, aimed at a literate elite; it was basically an educational tool sprung from the school and seminary tradition.

At the same time, however, there were stirrings in that other tradition—the popular, vulgar theatre of vaudeville and coarse humour which not even the combined forces of church and university had been able to stamp out. Radio had come along, and brought with it a realization that the Québecois thought, acted and spoke differently from the Frenchman, and that the long-buried dramatic arts might be more than an educational device: they might help a people to discover its soul.

During the nineteen-thirties several personalities emerged from the loudspeaker to become popular stars in Quebec. But the one who most clearly caught the heart of the public was a cocky, tough, shrewd *gamin* called Fridolin, who seemed to personify the little man of the province. Undetachable from his sling-shot, dressed in a beaten-up cap, a moth-eaten *Canadien* hockey sweater and filthy sneakers, the teen-aged Fridolin was the invention of Gratien Gélinas, born in 1909 in the small town of Saint-Tite de Champlain. In 1938 he put Fridolin on the stage in Montreal, in the first of ten annual "Fridolinons," satirical revues impishly devoted to what neither the French, the Americans nor the English-Canadians could do—carving up the family. And he wrote and performed in an outrageously colloquial Montreal dialect—thumbing his pug nose at everything proper, including the language of the Académie Française.

Fridolin made Gélinas the most popular native star in the history of Canadian entertainment. But he had more important things in mind: "Inspired by a love of the stage and by a faith in our national future," he was working, he later said, "to establish 'chez nous' an indigenous form of theatrical expression."

From one of his Fridolin sketches he developed a whole play: *Tit-Coq* (Li'l Rooster)—and with the astonishing success of *Tit-Coq* in 1948 the modern Canadian theatre announced its twenty-first birthday. It ran for an unprecedented nine months in Montreal in French, had substantial engagements in English (with a mostly French-Canadian cast) in Montreal and Toronto, was well received in Chicago, and then—and more of this later— was an instant flop on Broadway. The play was made into a film, and has been produced onstage in Sweden and Finland.

Tit-Coq is an orphan, a bastard, and a private in a war he neither understands nor cares about. Taken home for Christmas by a pal, he finds a substitute family and falls in love with the pal's sister, Marie-Ange. Desperately conscious of his illegitimacy, when the summons to go overseas arrives he does not marry her: abandoned before birth by his own father, he wants to be there when his son is born. While he is overseas, the months of separation becoming years, Marie-Ange is tormented into marrying a more available and secure suitor. Tit-Coq returns to find she still loves him and not her husband, who in turn has been drafted. They are about to go away together; but the Padré, who has seen Tit-Coq through both war and love, reminds them that for Marie-Ange divorce is impossible under Quebec law, and that any child of the union would be—like Tit-Coq himself—another bastard. Heart-broken, Tit-Coq goes off in a loneliness he knows will always possess him.

What might strike anyone about the play, first of all, is its cheek-by-jowl compound of sharp comedy and pathos—a mixture more akin to O'Casey or Chaplin than to any French or American playwright. The style might be called "selective realism" by a theoretician, but like Tit-Coq himself it owes little to its ancestors in Europe or America, aside from its general characteristics. The skill with which Gélinas draws the happy home of Marie-Ange, for example, avoids sentimentality by lacing the treacle with lemon bitters; I know of no scene quite like it. The piety of the maiden Aunt is real, but Gélinas is always needling it: speaking of the nice weather, she adds "If it keeps up, we shall have a beautiful Month of the Dead this year."

But for a Canadian, whether French- or English-speaking, the most striking aspect of the play is its recognizability. When the curtain rose in Toronto—the very Court of English-speaking Canada—the first scene was greeted with applause, not for the modest symmetry of the setting but from the sheer shock of familiarity. That room in a military camp, with its cedar walls and Quebec heater, was neither American nor European but decidedly Canadian. The family parlour which followed, with its "walls of grooved planks decorated with family portraits; old-fashioned stuffed furniture with small crochet-work doilies; plaited rug" and all, confirmed the unaccustomed identification.

In brief, Gélinas had succeeded in uniting the stage with its audience. "That is what I did," he later explained, "having come to the conclusion that the purest dramatic form—I don't say the only but the purest—would be that which displays as directly as possible the very audience to which the theatre addresses itself."

The direct aim at the Canadian audience meant, as he knew, risking a miss elsewhere. And the failure of the play on Broadway, where it was taken by the author's own company of Canadian actors, had a salutary effect on the whole Canadian theatre. Whereas before most Canadians would lamely have assumed they must have been mistaken in their judgment, this time they were able to muster the self-confidence to stand up for it. What made this possible for the first time were the particular faults which the New York critics picked upon. They found the Quebec-accented English (so familiar to us) hard to follow; too bad—but we knew that Americans did not alter their speech just because the English found it hard to follow. Then they considered the play's resolution—the acceptance of the impossibility of divorce—"contrived" and "theatrical"; too bad—but we knew that in the play's context any *other* resolution would have been contrived and theatrical. In brief, if they failed to appreciate it, that was no reason for us to abandon our own yardstick. We were already twenty-one.

But in *Tit-Coq* Gélinas did more than tell a story about a love-lorn little *Canadien* bastard. He told *the Canadien* story, about a people cut off long ago from their fatherland, trying desperately to find an identity in a bewildering world in which others hold the strings of power. Gélinas himself denies that any such parallel was in his mind when he wrote the play, and that in fact it was first drawn to his attention by a psychiatrist friend after the play opened. In any case it is there; and perhaps the very fact that it is unpremeditated adds to its prophetic force. At one point in *Tit-Coq* the following exchange takes place:

PADRE: Do you know what you remind me of, Tit-Coq? A branch torn off an apple tree by a storm. If it is left where it has fallen it will rot. But if it's picked up in time, it can be grafted onto another tree, and it will bear fruit, as if nothing ever happened.

TIT-COQ: Do you know something? You're not so dumb after all. We're sure going to replant it, that branch . . . and it's going to take root, because it's full of sap. And I promise you some damn fine apples.

In 1948, in the Canadian theatre, that was still only a promise.

In his next play, *Bousille and the Just,* written in 1959, Gratien Gélinas further tested his conviction that he could best achieve universality by probing his own roots. But this time he took the precaution of avoiding any twists in the plot which might, by the same token, preclude wider interest. *Bousille and the Just,* while based firmly in Quebec society, is primarily a play about man's inhumanity to man.

The story concerns a murder trial in Montreal. The ne'er-do-well son of the Gravel family (from Saint-Tite, Gélinas' home town) has killed a rival in a drunken brawl, and the family is determined to get him acquitted and save their shaky reputation. The sole witness is Bousille, a half-witted relative who runs errands for the Gravels. Deeply God-fearing, in savage contrast to the sanctimonious but grasping family, he is mercilessly tortured into perjuring himself. The son gets off, but the family's triumph is short-lived; robbed of his fragile self-respect, Bousille hangs himself in their barn, and they are called home to testify at an even grubbier inquest.

Once again Gélinas is dealing with the little man, the badgered innocent, and once again his characteristic counterpoint of derisive comedy and pathos gives the play its dramatic animation. In the sense that he is satirizing the religiosity of his own people ("les justes" in French means both "the righteous" and "the proper"), the play is regional. But in the sense that most of mankind pays lip-service to God while hotly courting Mammon, it is universal. Perhaps for this reason, *Bousille and the Just* has found a wider audience abroad than any of Gélinas' other plays, having been adapted for television in Britain, Czechoslovakia and West Germany as well as Finland.

Gélinas' third play—and his last to date—is *Yesterday the Children Were Dancing*, first produced in 1966. With it, he abandoned any thoughts of writing a work with international appeal, and boldly tackled the central *leitmotif* of the Canadian conscience, the conflict between French and English cultures. He succeeded in electrifying the nation in a way no other dramatist has done before or since. The timing was important. In 1967 Canada was to celebrate one hundred years of Confederation; keenly aware of the separatist volcano building up underneath the surface *bonhommie*, Gélinas used a Quebec family as a microcosm of the nation. With candour, biting irony and infinite compassion for those caught in the potential tragedy, he forced us to look at ourselves on the stage. It was the fulfilment of his search for "the purest dramatic form."

Pierre Gravel, a distinguished Montreal lawyer and devoted federalist ("but not under any and all conditions"), is offered a safe seat in Parliament, and a cabinet post, after the federal Minister of Justice suddenly dies. About to accept, he learns that his brilliant law-graduate son, André, is the leader of a terrorist gang dedicated to a separate State of Quebec. The bitter conflict which follows involves the whole family—and it is no mere ideological argument, because on André's acceptance or rejection of his father's rationale depends the setting-off of yet another bomb at a pre-scheduled time, as a result of which André will give himself up to the police. There is no real resolution for adamant father and headstrong son—only the mother's plea that "this is no time for insults . . . more than ever it's a time for love."

From the pathos of the lonely little bastard pitted against the world, and the irony of simple piety murdered by sanctimonious pretension, Gélinas has moved up the social scale. Now it is the turn of the *bourgeoisie*, because it is with them, he knows, that the future of Quebec now lies. The long intervals between the works of Gélinas (ten years, seven years) should not blind us to their links. All three of the plays are essentially tragic visions, relieved by stoic humour and a ray of hope. They show in common a profound faith in God alongside an earthy scorn for religiosity; a stubborn belief in man but a searing perception of his weaknesses; a level stance in a world filled with injustice which is, all the same, the only one we've got. Unlike some of his younger contemporaries in Quebec, Gélinas prescribes no political panaceas for the condition of man, there or elsewhere. He has remained a believer in federalism, *so long as* it allows the French-speaking Canadian to be himself in his own country; and he has worked tirelessly to bring about mutual understanding. But true to his own concept of a popular theatre, he uses the stage not to preach but to animate, to draw pictures and not conclusions. True also to a *form* of theatre with which he and his generation is familiar, he has refused to join the *avant-garde* fashionable elsewhere, whether Absurdist, Improvisational or Multi-media. This has led to his being considered old-fashioned in some quarters; to him it is simply a matter of being true to himself and not putting on someone else's airs.

Both his philosophy and his technique may, in fact, suggest a curious combination of American pragmatism and European existentialism—though the mixture will seem curious only to those who know little about Canada. For among us such compromises are a way of life, the *only* way we can come to terms with ourselves and with our neighbour on the continent. And a writer dedicated to putting his audience on the stage could scarcely avoid reflecting this salient aspect—indeed it is what most easily distinguishes a Canadian from an American or a European.

Recently Gélinas (now chairman of the state-funded Film Development Corporation) was asked what we should expect from the Canadian playwright. Characteristically he replied:

> He must not imitate others; he must write for himself from his roots. A Canadian writing for Broadway is as bad, as queer, as an American writing for a Quebec audience. Sentiment alone will not create a body of literature, a theatre. A literature expresses a nation which has found its personality. A man must marry—he needs children of his own, a family; fathers, brothers and relatives are not enough.

38

Gélinas has had many disciples in Quebec, the most prominent of whom is probably Marcel Dubé, who parlayed an overnight success with his first long play, *Zone,* into a prolific career as a dramatist. Like Gélinas, he has always written in a realistic vein about Quebec life, but with more emphasis on the dispiriting limitations of his society, and in a less biting, more elegiac style. His themes, however, are universal: the struggle of the young to get free, and of the old to accept their imprisonment.

It was not until the arrival of Michel Tremblay on the Montreal scene in 1948 that Gélinas' advice to "write Canadian" was taken literally by an angry young man unwilling to settle for less. In his *Les Belles-soeurs* he put onstage a gaggle of depressed and suppressed working-class women and let them tear each other to shreds in *joual,* the language of the streets. In one blow he shattered the comfortable myth of saintly *habitant* motherhood, shook theatrical tradition by importing the techniques of Genet, Arabal, Beckett and Albee, and shocked the improvers who wanted the world to think Montrealers spoke the world's French. Temblay has continued to shock, and in particular to insist on *joual*—a dialect as idiosyncratic as, say, thick Cockney or Brooklynese—as the only fitting one for his characters. In brief, he is carrying Gélinas' principle to its logical extreme, and exposing both its virtues and its vices—among the latter being sheer inaccessibility to audiences not in the know.

There are those who think the use of *joual* justified in the circumstances of Tremblay's inexorable realism but limited to that; those who consider it "THE turning point in the history of Quebec theatre"; and those who believe it is marching the theatre down a blind alley. Gratien Gélinas, who first launched colloquial Quebec French on its headlong stage career but refrained from following it all the way, recognizes it—but only as one of the children in his family. And all of the children recognize him as their father—which is all that Tit-Coq could have wished.

Gratien Gélinas in the title role of his play Tit-Coq, *with Huguette Oligny as Marie-Ange.*

EXTRACT FROM *TIT-COQ* BY GRATIEN GELINAS

Tit-Coq is a private in the Canadian Army, stationed in a training camp before being shipped overseas. He has a fight with his good friend Jean-Paul Désilets, who called him a "bastard" without realizing it was all too true. They are both brought up on charge, but the Commanding Officer's inclination to put them both in the "brig" is tempered by the fact that the Christmas leave is coming up. And when the Padré suggests that the one with the family (Jean-Paul) invite the other home for Christmas, the Commanding officer agrees to "wipe the slate," and Tit-Coq goes off to St. Anicet. He finds the family he had always wanted for himself, and falls in love with Jean-Paul's sister, Marie-Ange. This is the second scene of the First Act.

The Désilets' parlour, furnished with the taste and means of a working class couple settled for thirty years in the village of St. Anicet: walls of grooved planks decorated with family portraits; old-fashioned stuffed furniture with small crochet-work doilies; plaited rug; rack full of ornaments, souvenirs, etc. Left, on back panel, rises a turning stairway, its steps covered with habitant rug. On right panel, the parlour doorway, wide and decorated with scrolls, leads to an unseen hallway which goes to the front door and the kitchen. On the left panel, a bedroom door. A few Christmas decorations lend the whole room a touch of festivity and welcome. The stage is empty. A violent thumping is heard from the knocker of the front door, which opens offstage. JEAN-PAUL appears, right, haversack on his shoulder.

JEAN-PAUL:
Momma! *(Glances into the kitchen, then runs up a few stairway steps)* Momma.

FATHER:
(Coming from the bedroom, shirt in hand) Ah ben! morsac! (Shouts, right) Rosanna, here they are!

JEAN-PAUL:
Hello, Dad!

FATHER:
Hello, Jean-Paul! *(They fall into each other's arms.)*

JEAN-PAUL:
(as MOTHER comes down stairway) Hello, Momma! *(Runs to kiss her)*

FATHER:
(to MOTHER) I told you they'd be bouncing in tonight.

JEAN-PAUL:
(to TIT-COQ who has appeared in the parlour doorway, bashful, cap and haversack in hand) Come on over! *(Goes and puts arm around his shoulders)* Tit-Coq, meet my Mom and Dad. *(To FATHER)* My friend, Arthur St. Jean.

FATHER:
(shaking hands with TIT-COQ) Good evening, Mr. St. Jean. Glad to know you.

JEAN-PAUL:
Momma, I want you to meet— *(Notices she is wiping away a tear)* Aw, Mom, don't cry: we're not going, we're coming.

MOTHER:
I just can't help it.

FATHER:
(to TIT-COQ) Always the same story: if the cat takes a stroll in the lane, Mother has to bawl when he comes back!

MOTHER:
(nose in apron, to TIT-COQ) Excuse me, Mr . . . . Who is it, again?

JEAN-PAUL:
His name is Arthur St. Jean: but we call him Tit-Coq in camp, because he's gentle like a lamb.

FATHER:
Well, get your things off! *(To TIT-COQ, while the visitors are doing so)* Big crowd on the train, I suppose?

42

TIT-COQ:

(bashful) Oh yes . . .

JEAN-PAUL:

We had to stand as far as Valleyfield. And the train was ninety minutes late on top of that.

MOTHER:

(Her good spirits having returned) We nearly gave up holding supper for you. I told your father: "They must have taken the seven-thirty express."

FATHER:

That's why you catch me with my pants down.

JEAN-PAUL:

Anyway, we're sure glad to be here, eh, Tit-Coq?

TIT-COQ:

Oh yes . . .

FATHER:

Give me your things: I'll hang them up.

JEAN-PAUL:

Leave it to me. I know the place!

FATHER:

No, no! You're a guest now, too. *(He goes out a moment to hang the overcoats in the hallway.)*

MOTHER:

Take a seat, Mr. St. Jean. My, it's nice to see you home, both of you!

FATHER:

(to TIT-COQ) We were mighty pleased this morning when Jean-Paul telephoned you were coming.

MOTHER:

(who has seated herself before TIT-COQ) Of course, you'd rather be among your own folks. We'll do our best to take their

43

place, but I'm sure you're going to miss them. *(TIT-COQ coughs to hide his embarassment.)*

FATHER:
(to TIT-COQ) You wouldn't be related to the St. Jeans of these parts?

TIT-COQ:
(wretched) Oh! no . . .

MOTHER:
Your family must live awful far away if you can't go there for Christmas.

JEAN-PAUL:
(coming to TIT-COQ'S rescue) Uh, Tit-Coq is an orphan, Momma.

MOTHER:
(to TIT-COQ) No father or mother? *(TIT-COQ stutters a vague agreement.)* Why you poor boy. Isn't that dreadful! *(Moved to tears)* Well, you can be sure we're going to look after you, like you were one of our own.

FATHER:
(to change an awkward subject) Say, Jean-Paul: what about Marie-Ange and Aunt Clara? They were not on the train with you?

JEAN-PAUL:
No. I called Marie-Ange at noon; but Leopold Vermette was bringing them up in his car with his sister. They left at three o'clock; should be here any minute.

FATHER:
Well, before anybody else turns up, excuse me, I'm going to put on my shirt. Then we'll have a little drink to celebrate! *(He enters the bedroom)*

JEAN-PAUL:
I'm going to look the house over. *(He disappears right)*

MOTHER:
(makes conversation with TIT-COQ, who listens red-eared) We were talking about my sister-in-law and my youngest daughter. They're coming for the holidays . . . with a young man from the village who's working in Montreal too. Marie-Ange is her father's darling; he's dying to see her. Ah! to tell the truth, we hated to let her go last fall: only, they pay so well in town these days. Not that we worry about her over there. Oh no! I don't say it because she is my baby: but Marie-Ange is a good girl. Young Vermette who brings them, I think he's got an eye on her; but my little girl isn't so anxious: she says there's time enough for such foolishness.

JEAN-PAUL:
(coming from the kitchen) Momma, where' s the dog?

MOTHER:
You know, Fred stopped in just now: they must have left one behind the other, as usual. *(To TIT-COQ, while JEAN-PAUL goes poking around upstairs)* Fred' s my oldest; he's the blacksmith at the other end of the village. He might drop in with his wife, before midnight mass. Then there's my daughter, Claudia, and her husband. They are coming tomorrow morning from Arvida. They're bringing the baby. Imagine, she wanted to leave him home! "Poor Mother," she wrote. "It'll be too much bother for you." But I wrote back: "Bring him! If this goes on, Jesus-Mary, he'll have a beard, that child, and we'll hardly know him! "

FATHER:
(comes out of the bedroom buttoning up vest) There she goes again: blowing about her children! *(To TIT-COQ)* But no chance she'd ever talk about her old man!

An automobile horn honks outside.

JEAN-PAUL:
(comes downstairs) Here they are! *(He runs toward the street door)*

MARIE-ANGE:
(enters in a gust of wind) Hello, everybody!

45

FATHER:
Come here so I can kiss you.

MARIE-ANGE:
Hello, Dad! *(She throws herself into his arms.)*

FATHER:
Crée belle chouette! My, your cheeks are cold!

MARIE-ANGE:
(sparkling with joy) It was chilly in the car. Hello, Mummy!
(She kisses her.)

MOTHER:
Have a nice trip?

MARIE-ANGE:
All right as far as St. André; but then Leopold had to put on the
chains. *(She takes off her coat: little knitted cardigan over her
dress.)*

MOTHER:
You had your woolly drawers on, I hope?

MARIE-ANGE:
(blushing) Of course!

FATHER:
Where's your auntie?

MARIE-ANGE:
Outside, thanking Leopold Vermette; practically on her knees
to him . . . Although she did nothing but that all the way here!

MOTHER:
You didn't ask him in for a minute?

MARIE-ANGE:
He says he hasn't time: wants to get home for supper.

AUNT enters right, soundly muffled up.

46

MOTHER:
Hello, Clara, how are you?

AUNT:
My feet are frozen up to the navel! Good Lord! Here I am tramping up the place with my rubbers on. *(She returns toward the front door where she will take off her rubbers.)*

MOTHER:
(going after her) Oh, don't bother! The floor's not that clean . . . *(She disappears into the hallway following AUNT. They will be heard gossiping.)*

FATHER:
(introducing MARIE-ANGE to TIT-COQ, who had stepped out of the way) Marie-Ange, I think you know everybody here except Mr. St. Jean, alias Tit-Coq, who has just come with Jean-Paul.

MARIE-ANGE:
(to TIT-COQ) How do you do, Mr. St. Jean? So you're going to spend Christmas with us?

TIT-COQ:
(bashful) Oh yes . . .

MARIE-ANGE:
Get ready: you're going to have fun! *(Head in the clouds)* Oh, I was so anxious for today to come: I've been dreaming about it for three weeks. *(She goes upstairs with her coat.)*

FATHER:
(giving her a pat on the behind) Me, I was in no hurry, not a bit! *(Putting his arm around TIT- COQ'S shoulder, as the AUNT has just entered)* Now brace yourself: you're going to meet my sister! *(Leads him before AUNT)* Clara, this is Mr. St. Jean.

AUNT:
Happy to meet you, Mr. St. Jean.

FATHER:
(teasingly to TIT-COQ) Her, she's a fanatical Child of Mary!

47

Pretends she's in the city doing needlework, but that may be just a blanket for her real occupation . . . You're big enough to understand? I'm the eldest of the family, so she comes to fatten up at my expense every Christmas.

AUNT:
(To TIT-COQ) Don't listen to him. He must have started into his whisky blanc.

FATHER:
Morsac! That reminds me we need a drink. *(To TIT-COQ, indicating the AUNT)* Watch her take a dive into the sacramental wine! *(He goes out toward the kitchen.)*

MOTHER comes downstairs, followed by MARIE-ANGE. She has been taking the AUNT'S effects to the floor above.

MOTHER:
He's the same old tease, you know!

AUNT:
So I see! I think he's even more crazy than ever.

JEAN-PAUL:
(entering, a valise in either hand) Momma, where do I put their Ladyships' bags?

MOTHER:
Right upstairs. Take up Mr. St. Jean's things as well. You two will sleep in the boys' room. *(To TIT-COQ, while JEAN-PAUL is going up)* You'll have the bed of our son Rodolphe before he got married.

FATHER:
(returning with glasses and setting them on the table) Ah yes, our son Rodolphe, since he got married, it's terrible how he sleeps out!

MOTHER:
(to AUNT) You, Clara—

AUNT:
I suppose I'll stay in the girls' room, as usual?

48

MOTHER:
That's right. Only I wonder if all the beds are changed.

AUNT:
Don't worry: I'll see to that. *(She goes up.)*

MOTHER:
(seated comfortably on her behind) The sheets are in the closet at the top of the stairs.

MARIE-ANGE:
(coming back from the kitchen, doughnut in hand) Mummy, you've changed the kitchen curtains.

MOTHER:
It was about time. And it makes something new in the house for Christmas. *(She shouts toward the stairway.)* Clara, open the spare room, so it can warm up for Claudia tomorrow.

MARIE-ANGE:
You don't say they're coming?

MOTHER:
Oh yes, imagine! Her letter says tomorrow morning.

MARIE-ANGE:
Not with little Jackie?

FATHER:
(serving drinks) Sure! They're bringing the baby, so we can eat a slice of him.

MARIE-ANGE:
The little cabbage, I'm dying to see him! I've brought him the sweetest little angora sweater . . .

FATHER:
(to JEAN- PAUL, who was about to go upstairs again with his and TIT-COQ'S haversacks) Jean-Paul, knock off a minute and have a drink with us. *(He gives him a little glass of whisky, and one to TIT-COQ.)* Your good health!

JEAN-PAUL:

And yours!

TIT-COQ:

(bashful) And yours.

FATHER:

To Christmas: when we don't have to hide to take a drink. *(They drink.)* Good! Now, Mummy, quit loafing and serve supper. I got a hole in my stomach.

MOTHER:

(rising and moving toward the kitchen) It won't be long: everything's ready.

MARIE-ANGE:

(taking her MOTHER'S arm) I'm coming with you.

MOTHER:

Mind you don't spoil your new dress. You know, in the kitchen today . . . *(She disappears, right, as JEAN-PAUL goes up with his haversacks.)*

FATHER:

(left alone with TIT-COQ, puts an arm around his shoulder) Listen, my boy, you didn't talk much since you came in: "Oh yes," "Oh no." Of course you're among people you don't know, but you better loosen up as quick as you can, eh? If you spend five days holding yourself in like that, you're going to be sick! To start with, this calling you Mr. St. Jean, it's finished: we're going to call you Tit-Coq, like the rest. And you'll see we're not at all stuffy. For one thing, we're not rich nor extremely intelligent! We're just an ordinary working family in the village of St. Anicet. Oh, yes, to put you at ease right away: in case you need to go there, one of these days, . . . *(Points it out with his finger)* . . . it's upstairs, the second door on the left. Another thing, maybe we don't count for much, but we like each other just the same, all of us together. So don't be scared. During Christmas, we get to cuddling and kissing, like a bunch of calves sucking ears, right to the fourth generation on either side! Aunts with whiskers, there's plenty of them, I warn you! Then again, I've got some pretty nice nieces.

MARIE-ANGE:
(an apron over her dress, has entered and cries from the stair-way landing) Jean-Paul! Auntie! Supper's ready!

FATHER:
(continuing to TIT-COQ) Now let's go and eat. If you're bashful at the table, you'll go away skinny. But if you don't wait to be served, you'll get a fat belly; because Mother Désilets, she didn't invent the telephone, but for good cooking she can't be beat . . .

MARIE-ANGE:
(putting her arm around her FATHER'S waist) Daddy, it's ready!

JEAN-PAUL comes downstairs and goes out toward the kitchen.

FATHER:
(to TIT-COQ, indicating MARIE-ANGE) A fine bit of girl, don't you think? *Crée belle chouette, va!* Too bad we're poor. If I was rich, I'd pay your wages and keep you home with me.

While the AUNT is coming downstairs, all three move toward the kitchen, the FATHER with his arms around the shoulders of MARIE-ANGE and TIT-COQ.

FATHER:
(to his "CHOUETTE," while they walk) At least, you've brought me a present, eh? If not, I warn you; there's no place for you in the house . . . and you'll sleep in the snow tonight, *morsac!*

The curtain falls.

4 James Reaney

In the second half of the twentieth century, Canada has produced two internationally famous scholars in the fields of literature and communications media: Northrop Frye and Marshall McLuhan. Frye, first with his exploration of Blake's symbolic universe in *Fearful Symmetry,* then in his influential *Anatomy of Criticism,* established the claim of the artistic imagination to be judged by its own inner rules. McLuhan used an artist's imagination to probe our technological society, demonstrated how we advance precariously by looking into a "rear-view mirror," and sought fresh insights through playthings such as card and word games. One of the interesting Canadian mysteries is why so few of our playwrights—in comparison with writers elsewhere—seem to have been swayed by their liberating ideas.

The important exception is James Reaney. It would be a disservice to Reaney to suggest that he simply swallowed the notions of Frye or McLuhan (or anyone else) and regurgitated them as drama; although he studied English at the University of Toronto while they were teaching there, he took no courses from them. And while his debt to Frye's writings has been acknowledged, his connection with McLuhanism is more coincidental. Reaney is, moreover, a poet and a novelist as well as a playwright, and the influences on him have been many and varied; in sum, he is a highly original artist, working a territory so unlike anyone else's that one critic calls it simply "Reaney-land."

James Reaney was born in 1926, near Stratford, Ontario. Not only the countryside and the small town stayed in his blood, but also its fundamentalist religion (all hellfire-and-brimstone), its closeted family skeletons, its games, its toys, its songs, its very nursery rhymes. Seldom has a writer made fuller use of his own unremarkable childhood, and seldom has a childhood provided the raw materials for so many remarkable variations. Except for the atypical *Three Desks* (his only play mostly in prose), all his published works seem based on childhood memories—and yet none of them is merely either autobiographical or documentary. It is as though he insists on the superior clarity and vitality of a child's perception of adults, seen as personifying huge forces to which we can give only unsatisfactory abstract names, but which we know deeply from the time we sense anything. What Reaney succeeds in doing is to weave rich universal myths out of homespun.

He published poetry while still at college, and also one shocking short story which earned him the enviable reputation of a literary delinquent. A first novel showed symptoms of Beardsley's disease: bizarre artificiality. He was then obviously wrestling with an old problem: a burgeoning imagination which outran the real world of his experience, but which yet had little design of its own. Already widely read, he found himself challenging the giants of literature, and was caught in a dilemma common to all artists working, like Canadians, out of the mainstream: should he copy them or try to find his own way? It was at this time, apparently, that Reaney absorbed Frye's *Fearful Symmetry*, which provided him with the answer. He would borrow Blake's formula, but produce his own vision:

> To see a World in a grain of sand,
> And Heaven in a wild flower,
> Hold Infinity in the palm of your hand,
> And Eternity in an hour.

He could have it both ways. From *his* sand, *his* flower, *his* hand, *his* hour, he would fashion a whole new universe. To do so, he needed what he called a "symbolic grammar" of his own, to describe his own "literary geography"; he had to take the ordinary things in his memory-bag—colours, plants, animals, words, events—and turn them into giant-size resonators. The elementary had to be made elemental, the simple must become symbol. The pattern they made would then be his and all men's at one and the same time.

Thus Reaney answered in a different way one of the main questions that traditionally plagues Canadian writers: "Who am I?" Instead of searching for his identity in his environment or hoping that by recording it he would define himself, he meant to fracture the environment and from the fragments build whatever identity he liked. With tiles loosed from the old mosaic he would re-create "the backbone of a person growing up, leaving home, going to big cities, getting rather mixed up and then not coming home again but making home and identity come to wherever he is." For this reason his plays all present a strange double image to our eyes: we recognize the pieces, but the whole picture is powerful strange. It's Southern Ontario, right enough—that's the very way they speak and dress and act (or did a generation ago)—but how did it get all mixed up with Olympus and King Arthur, with Paradise and Purgatory, with Sodom and Gomorrah, with Grimm's Fairy Tales? In Reaney-land they play tricks with the rear-view mirrors: life seems to imitate art.

You can see what he's up to with the prologue to his first full-length play, *The Rules of Joy,* entered in a 1958 competition for the Stratford Shakespeare Festival. The astonished audience was to have been addressed thus:

> Shall I tell you a story of the jealous Moor or of the old king and his three daughters? No. I shall tell you a story of myself when fifteen years ago I was sixteen. It happened in my father's kingdom. His kingdom was the realm of love where people learned the rules of joy. I can see that summer in my father's house. Summer in the village, in the church, in the fields, those roads, the people I summon to appear and myself as then out of the lake of time and death—come up!

The play won no award, and Reaney rewrote it, rechristening it *The Sun and the Moon.* Although not produced on the stage until after his next play, *The Killdeer, The Sun and the Moon* gives us the first clear picture of the topography of the unusual kingdom about which Reaney would continue to write.

An old tramp "like a dwarf in a fairy-tale" curses the manse of the Reverend Kingbird, in the Village of Millbank. Widower Kingbird with his teen-age son Andrew and daughter Susan, are beset by an itinerant evangelist named Mrs. Shade and her "son" (the product, she claims, of a long-ago liaison with Kingbird). This young man confesses to Susan that his "mother" is actually an abortionist on-the-run from Toronto. But Mrs. Shade's accusations take root among the town gossips, who drive the Reverend from town. Mrs. Shade attempts to confirm her supernatural gifts by drugging young Andrew and pretending to raise him from the dead. But the powers of good rally, the evil Mrs. Shade slinks away when confronted by the Reverend's real light-o'-love, the tramp is routed and all ends happily.

If this plot summary fails to do the play justice, neither does it include the full inventory of melodramatic conceits—among which one may find falsified documents, a put-back clock, an incriminating diary, a hollow tree, a coffin, a castrated cat, and more sudden switches than a political convention. None of these, however, is unintentionally funny (Reaney knows how to be both biting and hilarious when he wants), and all of them make sense once the laws of the country, like those of Alice's Wonderland, are understood. If one wants credibility one finds it not in the plot or the characters, but in the internal consistency of an imagination turned inside out, the unconscious (as it were) made visible. There is no lack of accurate observation of ordinary life here; we know this town and its people well. But we are used to seeing surfaces, and to recognizing surface plausibility in our theatres. Reaney is after a different kind of truth—the kind which binds us, instinctively, to the persistent myths of mankind: light and dark, creativity and sterility, life and death. He sees no reason why these primordial dramatic conflicts should not go on in the breast of Andrew Kingbird of Millbank, Ont., as well as in those of the Biblical heroes and Gothic heroines with whom Andrew grew up. What, indeed, could be more "natural"?

It was not *The Sun and the Moon*, however, which first introduced Reaney to the theatre-going public, but his next play, *The Kildeer*, in 1960. Its structure (except for a third act which went through several later revisions) was more assured, and its characters less black and white—even though the author had added murder, corpse-mutilation and homosexuality to his stratagems. But what struck audiences at once (aside, no doubt, from the novel dramaturgy) was the stream of soaring, spinning, whirling, flashing words which poured from the stage. The accent was unmistakeably Southern Ontario ("the saft" for "this afternoon"; "Hark to them dratted birds"; "the whole room's real pretty"; "the daughter of the Royal Bank of Canada's this branch's manager," etc.), and so were the piety, the hypocrisy, the petty vanity, the emotional constipation. Poet Reaney had, for the first time in our theatre, distilled our raw Ontario dialect into a genuine *aqua vitae*; drunk on it, his characters revealed the potent depths they tried so hard to conceal when sober. But this satiric portrait was only half the picture; the other half was more clearly seen by the British critics (when it was later performed in Glasgow), who knew nothing of its Ontario original.

Harry Gardner is grudgingly living in Stratford with his over-protective mother, and wants to marry Rebecca, the egg-girl. His mother pushes him at Vernelle, who has money. Mrs. Gardner is visited by Madam Fay, a travelling cosmetic sales-woman, drifting back to her home town trailing echoes of a scandalous past: years ago she had run off with her foster-sister's husband (Rebecca's parents), only to be pursued by her own husband, who shot her lover, her sister and her two sons, and then himself. Harry marries Vernelle; Rebecca marries Madam Fay's half-wit son Eli, and later is accused of murdering his guardian (and lover?) Clifford Hopkins. In the play's first version, she pleads guilty and is imprisoned. Harry, returning from law-school in Toronto, his marriage a failure, sets out to get her off: he sleeps with her in her cell to make her pregnant so she cannot legally be hanged. At the trial, the mystery of Clifford's death is eventually solved by the intervention of a singular doctor-hermit, who seems to know everything. It develops that Rebecca is innocent; it is Madam Fay who has tried to ruin all their lives, motivated by girlhood jealousy of her step-sister, whose pet killdeer she once coveted. (In a second published version—with the complications much reduced along with the number of sets—the imprisonment and trial are omitted.)

The killdeer is "the bird that flies in over the town, crying its name when it's going to rain," and also acts as decoy to draw enemies away from its nestlings. But that is only one of a host of interlocking symbols which Reaney presents in this story of a young man's emancipation from "home." Madam Fay (Morgan la Fay?), obviously another Mrs. Shade, is the passionate evil in all of us, the angel of death, a vulture. In fact each of the humans has a bird or animal character. The remarkable vitality of the play, despite its loquacity, lies in this tension between the natural and the symbolic—between acutely reproduced colloquial speech and densely meaningful poetry, between small-scale physical actions and large-scale metaphysical reverberations.

Reaney's third long play, *The Easter Egg* (1962), is mainly notable for its repetition of the theme of a young man caught between Witch and Good Fairy, and for its increasing emphasis on the power of the word—for the Witch is trying to keep him (after a traumatic shock) mute and memoriless, while the Good Fairy eventually restores his power to speak, to name things. In the meantime Reaney had also written a short piece, *One-Man Masque*, composed mainly of a group of his poems, in which he abandoned this theme and devised a method of using simple, familiar objects symbolically to take us, poem by poem, through a whole lifetime:

> SCENE: The curtain rises to reveal a collection of objects arranged in a circle. Starting on the left we have a cradle, a baby carriage, a child's chair, a big chair, a table, a bed, a rocking chair and a coffin. This line of objects fills the extreme front of the stage. Now, starting near the coffin and circling back towards the cradle again, we have another line of objects: a hall tree, a rain barrel, a section of stairs, a dresser with a mirror, a tree branch, a ladder, a spinning wheel and a cardboard box . . .

The French theoretician Antonin Artaud had diagnosed the modern theatre's malaise as "a rupture between things and words, between things and the ideas and signs that are their representation"; the cure he proposed was to do away with conventional language altogether. But Reaney, as a poet, was committed to another remedy: he wanted to tie things and ideas and words even closer together, in a new metaphorical configuration, a new zodiac. The difficulty in his earlier plays, he found, was to convince audiences that the world he was presenting was not an embroidered real world but a transformed one. It was from his own childhood that he had drawn most of his dramatic materials, and it was among children that he found the readiest acceptance of the idea of a "make-believe" world, in which a ladder, for example, could become a skyscraper. In 1966 he started a Listener's Workshop in London, Ontario (where he now taught at the University of Western Ontario), and experimented with improvisation for children. From this emerged a work called *Listen to the Wind*, in which (as in an earlier children's play, *Names and Nicknames*) performers and audience joined in various kinds of games and presented a melo-dramatic play-within-the-play—using simple props and acting out themselves such elements as scenery and weather, often in song. The whole thing was "Let's Make-Believe"; and, as McLuhan would say, the medium was the message. From this he progressed to a longer work, in which he made it inescapably clear that the action took place inside a boy's head, "when he was sick with the measles at about ten years of age" and was kept in the dark. *There* the imagination could run riot!

Colours in the Dark was presented by the Stratford Festival, at its smaller Avon Theatre, in 1967. In his Author's Note, Reaney tells us why he called it "a play box":

> I happen to have a play box and it's filled with not only toys and school relics, but also deedboxes, ancestral coffin plates, in short a whole life. When you sort through the play box you eventually see your whole life—as well as all of life—things like Sunday School albums which show Elijah being fed by ravens, St. Stephen being stoned. The theatrical experience in front of you now is designed to give you that mosaic-all-things-happening-at-the-same-time-galaxy-higgledy-piggledy feeling rummaging through a play box can give you. But underneath the juxtaposition of coffin plate with baby rattle with Royal Family Scrapbook with Big Little Book with pictures of King Billy and Hitler—there is the backbone of a person growing up, leaving home, going to big cities, getting rather mixed up and then not coming home again but making home and identity

come to him wherever he is. The kids at the very end of the play manage to get their lightning rod up and attract the thunder that alone can waken the dead. Or on the other six hands, as Buddha says, there are any number of other interpretations that fit the mosaic we're (director, writer, actors, kids, designers, composer) giving you.

Colours in the Dark has forty-nine short scenes, onstage screens, a great many poems and songs, and an almost continuous sound and music accompaniment. The danger is that instead of getting a chance at a lottery rich in "any number of interpretations," we shall be given one—the director's; that he may turn it into a private multi-media exercise instead of an inducement to members of the audience to use their own imagination.

And here we come to the tricky corner into which all symbolists may paint themselves unless they leave an exit-path: the more personal and elaborate their cosmos becomes, the less accessible it is to all but disciples—either of the man or of occultism. The explorer of his own Wonderland is inviting others to go along on *his* ego-trip; if they are sufficiently fascinated, either by childhood in general, or this writer's childhood, or the symbolism involved, they will accept; if not, they will decline, even though (sometimes because) this implies that they are too stupid to know what's good for them. There is plenty of evidence that James Reaney is not writing out of self-therapy—that he is genuinely seeking a break-through to what Jung called the "collective unconscious": not only to a private preserve but also to a park we all may share. (The private preserves might well be represented by his opera libretti, *Night-blooming Cereus* especially, with which we do not have space to deal.) But he is nonetheless in danger of catering increasingly to a special and limited audience.

Paradoxically, therefore, Reaney's most lasting contribution to our theatre, so far, may not be at all the "symbolic grammar" and "literary geography" he set out to create, but the by-products: his transmutation of our dull speech to silver, our square behaviour to purple, and our fettered imaginations to all the colours of the rainbow.

A scene from Act One of The Killdeer *with Kate Reid as Madam Fay and Amelia Hall as Mrs. Gardner.*

EXTRACT FROM *THE KILLDEER* BY JAMES REANEY

The scene is the interior of Mrs. Gardner's cottage. "Mrs.
Gardner is a very fussy, matriarchal, pious, bossy, evangelical
type. Her visitor—the cosmetic saleswoman, Madam Fay—is
vital, pagan, and dressed in an elegant blouse with a dark skirt
stylishly gored in front." Mrs. Gardner recognizes Madam Fay,
from an old newspaper photograph, as the subject of a terrible
local scandal. Madam Fay refreshes her memory with the details.

MRS. GARDNER:
Oh, I can't believe it. I can't believe it at all.

MADAM FAY:
Whaddya mean you can't believe it, you can't believe that!
You're dying to believe it. You believed it
Even before my mouth ever opened. You bought
That pot of vanishing cream and those toenail scissors
So you could hear me and then say, 'I can't believe it! '
What in hell's name is it you don't believe?
You don't believe I ran off with my sister's husband?

MRS. GARDNER:
I believe it. I only said—I don't know what I said.

MADAM FAY:
You don't believe my husband went over and shot
My sister and most of her family then, and then
He shot himself and the other man went nuts
And my sister's girl is left and my puling boy,
Eli, who won't look me straight in the eye?

MRS. GARDNER:
That may very well be. It was all in the papers.

MADAM FAY:
Was it ever! Then you don't believe God won't
Forgive me. Is that it? Well, do you know why?
Because I pray to Him nightly: 'God, don't

Forgive me.' And he always answers prayers.
Do you believe that?

MRS. GARDNER:
Yes, that may very well be.

MADAM FAY:
And you like hearing it, don't you? That's my pitch
With you church-going biddies. You'd buy
The rouge pot Jezebel used the day she was tossed
Off her balcony to the dogs just to see
The woman that caused four deaths and one
Of the splatteriest nervous breakdowns I ever saw
And one blighted boy—my son—and one blighted girl—
My sister's daughter.

MRS. GARDNER:
We women are never all to blame. The men—

MADAM FAY:
Lorimer was a fool. He asked me, do you know why?
He was so much in love with his wife he wanted
Something from her only she could give. Her
Forgiveness for something. She always forgave
So lovely. So we ran away and somehow my husband
Guessed that it wasn't me Lorimer loved
But his own wife. So he killed the wife, her kids,
To spite Lorimer, me, himself, the whole world.
God! He knew what would really kill Lorimer.
And yet I can never figure out **how** he knew that.
He was not clever. My husband was not that clever.
That's extra. You'd better buy a thing more.
I don't usually do that scene. It tires me out.

MRS. GARDNER:
Are these hairpins? I'll have them. How much?

MADAM FAY:
That will cover it. Well, I've fixed you up.
You're beautiful now. By the way, when you tell
The ladies at your church about me, don't forget
I wasn't her real sister—they adopted me.

I was an orphan. And my husband didn't shoot
The little boys. No. He took the butt-end
Of the rifle and smashed their heads in.

MRS. GARDNER:
You don't carry combs, do you?

MADAM FAY
Hah! I do. But I won't let you have one. Next time!
And I had a fascinating girlhood too. Mm! Yum!
Next time! Say, who's the connoisseur around here?
Look at the time. Good day to you, ma'am.

*MADAM FAY leaves. MRS. GARDNER collapses and then
dashes to her window to see MADAM FAY's departure, then
goes out into the kitchen. Her clock strikes five. She re-enters
with tea things. HARRY enters with bicycle which he stores in
the kitchen, then sits down and takes off clips.*

MRS. GARDNER:
Harry, I wish you'd come in the back door with your
Bicycle. If a piece of mud dropped off it onto this
Floor I'd skin you.

HARRY:
Yes, Mother.

MRS. GARDNER:
Did anything interesting happen to you today?

HARRY:
No, nothing happened at the bank, Mother.

MRS. GARDNER:
Anything new on the way home?

HARRY:
I saw a funny pink car.
A Baby Austin. Pink! It said on it in red,
'Here comes Madam Fay'.

MRS. GARDNER:
That may very well be.

Here's your tea. Have it like a good boy. I'm just
On the verge of fixing you your supper.

HARRY:
That's just it, Mother. I won't be home for supper.
I can't stay home for supper—if it's
All right with you, Mother, that is.

MRS. GARDNER:
Where are you going for supper, Son?

HARRY:
No sugar, please, Mother.

MRS. GARDNER:
And what is wrong with my sugar, pray?

HARRY:
It's—it's what was causing my acne, Mother!
I went to a doctor. Dr. Smith. He said—

MRS. GARDNER:
And you never told me. Went to a doctor!

HARRY:
Why should I? Dr. Smith says, "Harry,
What are you eating? " So I told him.

MRS. GARDNER:
My home cooking.

HARRY:
Yes. I said to him, I eat Mother's home cooking.
Yes, all those pickled cherries, and candied pears,
Crystallized lemon rinds and glazed pumpkin blossoms,
Christmas puddings as big as a man's belly.

MRS. GARDNER:
Too big for yours, evidently.

HARRY:
You haven't seen my belly
Since I was sixteen. I can remember the last time

She saw me naked. Every Saturday night Mother used to
Wash me all over. To have a woman know all about you
From the time you're little!
She's even had you in her belly.

MRS. GARDNER:

My home cooking!
Well, you can just go and get married and get somebody
Else to—somebody else to cook for you. Oh!

*They rise and stand turned away from each other, only turning
when the speech is actually meant to be heard by the other.
For a few moments they idly turn in and out; sometimes their
glances coincide—sometimes not. Sort of a Harpo Marx
routine.*

HARRY:

Go ahead! Bawl! I'm past caring. I was your baby—

MRS. GARDNER:

Oh ducky, duck, duck, I used to dandle you—

HARRY:

But you're not my baby now. So don't cry.

MRS. GARDNER:

Who' s invited you to supper or am I ever to know?

HARRY:

If I could only get away! If I could get married!
I did go to old Mrs. Sow who charges fifty cents
Down under the railway cross-over but when
I was going to knock on the door I couldn't . . .
I kept thinking of Mother with her white apron.
Guess who's invited me to supper, Mother?

MRS. GARDNER:

Oh Son, why do you tease your old Mother so?
Sonny, I wish you'd open your heart to me
Show me your heart. We used to be so close.

HARRY:

You read my letters and diaries and my bank book

And my dirty linen. When I'm asleep
Why don't you take off the top of my head
And put your hand in? What could I show you
Mother, except yourself?

*They turn inwards to each other and outwards idly for a few
moments.*

Mother, if I tell you where I'm going to supper
Will you promise not to go berserk?

MRS. GARDNER:
I promise!

HARRY:
(pausing) Oh gosh! This room! This front parlour of yours!
I think I'll go mad if I don't get one day
Of my life when I don't come home to this.
Why don't I run away? Because I'm afraid,
Afraid of the look on a face I'd never see.
Dear old Mother's face! This room! This room!
These brown velvet curtains trimmed with
One thousand balls of fur! Fifteen kewpie dolls!
Five little glossy china dogs on a Welsh dresser!
Six glossy Irish beleek cats and seven glass
Green pigs and eight blue glass top hats and
Five crystal balls filled with snow falling down
On R.C.M.P. constables. Two little boys on chamber
Pots: Billy Can and Tommy Can't. That stove—
Cast-iron writhing and tortured curlicues!

MRS. GARDNER:
I think the whole room's real pretty!
I started it from nothing twenty-five years ago
And look at it now!

HARRY:
Look at it now!
This is your room, Mother. Your mind is like this.
It's where I've spent most of my life and it's not
Real pretty.

MRS. GARDNER:
That may very well be but who—

HARRY:
Mr. Coons, the bank manager. My boss. On short notice
He has invited me to dinner as he calls it.
A guest from out of town can't come so I'm invited
To come up to his place on Waterloo Crescent
Across the river at half past six tonight.

An electric pause.

MRS. GARDNER:
Oh son Harry, what an honour! Oh son Harry!
This is your big chance!

HARRY:
Big chance for what?

MRS. GARDNER:
You'll marry his daughter. I feel it here and here!

HARRY:
His daughter! I've never met her. She's too old.
I really think he just—

MRS. GARDNER:
Take that shirt off!
Take that coat off! I can smell your sweat from here!
A bath! A shave! Get into that bathroom!
There's plenty of hot water in the tank!
This great chance must not be missed!
Out of all the other young clerks at the bank!
Five of them—Mr. Coons invited you—**you**
To his home for supper—dinner. Oh, I hope
He doesn't tempt you with alcohol. Oh,
Nothing so wonderful since Queen Mary's carpet.
My son of humble birth to marry the daughter
Of the Royal Bank of Canada's this branch's
Manager! Into that bathtub, boy!

Blackout

5 George Ryga

Among the reasons often given for Canada's slowness in developing a dramatic literature are that it is a young country without traditions of its own; that consequently it has no myths; that its history, being evolutionary rather than revolutionary, is flat and dull; and that its amiably decent citizens provide few of the essential materials for conflict which more colourful societies have turned into exciting theatre. One writer who has never believed this is George Ryga. He considers them not reasons for backwardness but rationalizations for gutlessness.

Born in 1932 on a homestead in northern Alberta, of Ukrainian parentage, and self-educated after only seven years in a one-room school house, Ryga had his Western dukes up from the start. Full of myths, songs, stories and indignation enough for several writers, he turned out short stories, a novel and several radio and television plays before turning to the stage form in 1964. By that time the main elements of his approach, his thought and even his style were already evident. Folklore, both spoken and sung (Ryga writes the music to his own lyrics, many of which have been recorded). Intense sympathy with the individual, and equally intense hatred of the impersonal "system." A keen ear for the rhythms and cadences of the West's varied dialects. A profound respect for the power of nature and instinct, and an earthy disrespect for pedantry and artiness. A freewheeling dramatic pattern, evolved from his experience with the electronic media, in which events and anecdotes from past and present overlap and leapfrog—a cumulative mosaic rather than a progressive plot.

With his concern for the underdog, and his sensitivity to the conflict he saw around him, it was not unnatural that Ryga's first play was called, simply, *Indian*. For in the plight of Canada's first inhabitants lay drama aplenty.

The subject was hardly new. The very first play performed by the European newcomers on Canadian soil, *the Theatre of Neptune*—presented in 1605 by members of Champlain's settlement at Port Royal—included native chieftains in its cast; their roles were dignified and seemly, even if the purpose of their presence was to honour the King of France. Later theatrical productions under the French regime also employed native performers, but as "demons" to be saved by their enlightened Christian overlords. For over three centuries, in fact, the attitude of the whites toward the natives in Canada fell into one of three categories:

> The most obvious is a Darwinistic paternalism: the red man is doomed to assimilation by the incursion of Anglo-Saxons because he is unable to survive in competitive evolution; the white, however, is trying to do his best to make the death struggle of the primitive as soft as possible. The second view is that the Indians are noble savages, children of nature who have prowess, cunning and dignity, yet tend to be ignorant and slothful . . . The third conception is that the degenerate white has corrupted the Indian, but it is also an Anglo-Saxon virtue to raise the aboriginal to hitherto unprecedented levels of civilization and salvation, fashioned on the white model.[1]

These views are still common, but a fourth is gaining ground: that the native peoples must be allowed their own valuable civilization (which we have done our best to destroy, one way or another). Ryga's two plays about Indians have substantially contributed to this new attitude.

The first, *Indian*, has no solution to offer, but it puts the result of our political and social policies graphically on the

---

[1] R.G. Haycock, *The Image of the Indian*. Waterloo: Waterloo Lutheran University publication, 1971.

stage. It is a short play, the most uncomplicatedly naturalistic he has done, with but one event. A transient Indian labourer (we never know his real name) is found sleeping off a binge from the previous night, his tent burned down and his companions on a fence-making detail fled. His irate boss has plenty to say about no-good Indians, but warns him not to complain to the government agent who is expected shortly. The boss leaves. The starved and exhausted Indian drives himself to work again, but is interrupted by the arrival of the agent, a chatty do-gooder. Under threat of physical violence, the agent is forced to listen to a recital of the Indian's abysmal life. More frightened than his quarry, he finally drives off while the Indian stoically returns to work.

In this small tale we find the germs of most of the themes which Ryga has developed at greater length in his other published plays to date, *The Ecstasy of Rita Joe, Grass and Wild Strawberries*, and *Captives of a Faceless Drummer*—although only the first of these continues the Indian topic.

First of all, the setting is symbolic: "flat, grey, non-country." This no-place environment, with its intimations of homelessness, of rootlessness, is central to all Ryga's works; the Indian is a transient in his own country, even his temporary shelter demolished, his family life a shambles, his future existence leading nowhere. From this follows the equally typical motif of non-identity ("All Indians same—nobody")—which puts the "Made in Canada" stamp on these plays; the Indian baffles the agent by claiming three different names. Depersonalized and unconnected, a member of what Grattan O'Leary called "the society of neithers," he turns his anonymity into a weapon against the community which would label him without recognizing him: "I got no past . . . no future . . . nothing! . . . I dead! You get it? . . . I never been anybody. *I not just dead . . . I never live at all.*" Attempting to bring him to heel, the agent says "There are laws in this country. Nobody escapes the law!" That is the Indian's point: that being nobody is the only way of escaping the system of rules imposed by society. And the rules, finally, Ryga sees as the last resort not of the strong, but of the scared. "Whole world is scare," the Indian tells the agent: "It make you scare you should know too much about me."

All of these themes, as well as Ryga's technique of lifting the past into the foreground so that the present becomes a kind of hallucination, are developed more fully in *The Ecstasy of Rita Joe* (1967). This is a much more ambitious play, a sort of vicious circle played out on a circular stage, in which Ryga adds song, dance, mime and lighting effects to his bag of theatrical tricks. The icing might, in less sincere and sturdy hands, have sunk the cake—as indeed some critics claim it did. But the play had strong impact in Vancouver, Ottawa and Montreal, in the latter in a French translation by Gratien Gélinas—a great compliment, since it marked the sole occasion on which Quebec's leading playwright has translated the work of an English-Canadian playwright.

Rita Joe, a native girl come from the Cariboo to find work in Vancouver, is the one caught in the vicious circle. She is on trial—for prostitution, for vagrancy, for petty theft; the trials are confused—what does the charge matter? She is in love with Jamie Paul, who dreams of mounting an industry for his people but wastes both time and energy in empty bravado against the whites while he guzzles their booze. Her old father, a sage who finds serenity in acceptance of adversity, begs her to come home to the reservation; but even if she could leave the city (which one law or another always seems to prevent her from doing), she is now of the "society of neithers"—home is nowhere. Jamie is killed by a train (the symbol of what killed the Indian way of life), and Rita Joe is almost ritually raped and murdered at the play's end: the "ecstasy" of a martyr. An echo of society's self-righteousness comes from one of the rapers, who cannot understand what all the fuss is about—"We hardly touched her."

Whereas *Indian* consisted of one incident, *The Ecstasy of Rita Joe* abounds in them. The nominal setting is the court-room, but it is backed by a "mountain cyclorama," and in front of that "a darker maze curtain to suggest gloom and confusion, and a city-scape." And the trial is only a coat-tree for remembered incidents as they arise in the minds of those there, often out of chronological order. A line of dialogue in the trial becomes part of another scene, the end of which then returns us to the trial. Transitions are sometimes abrupt, sometimes gradual. We never get the whole story, only fragmentary highlights—the relationship between which we do not fully grasp until the whole mosaic is in place. This is, as Brian Parker has pointed out, the form of the *folk ballad*. And Ryga introduces here an element used increasingly in plays to come: the interlocked, or interlocutory, song cycle. Sometimes the songs actually drive the action forward; sometimes they heighten a mood, or provide a bridge from one mood to the next. More often the singer is an outsider, who—as is the case with *Rita Joe's* "liberal white folklorist with a limited concern and understanding"—forces the audience to see the action through a mediating filter. This "distancing" device, as Brecht had shown earlier, allows a playwright to confront the audience directly with the blame for what is shown: they can, however shamefacedly, identify with the "liberal" singer if not with the victims.

"I was amazed," wrote Chief Dan George of the Burrard Tribe, who first played Rita Joe's father, "at the reaction the play received in Ottawa. People came to see us to say that now, for the first time, they understood a little of what the Native Peoples have suffered and are suffering." It was 362 years since the *Theatre of Neptune*.

For his next play, *Grass and Wild Strawberries* (1969), Ryga turned to another aspect of the life around him: the conflict between the nature-loving hippy generation and its rule-bound, city-wracked parents. The generation gap might seem even more of a hackneyed dramatic subject than Indians; but once again, Ryga was not interested in the obvious. His play is really another variation on the theme of going home, of finding oneself. Susan, a genuine *ingénue,* is living in a commune with Allan, a young painter who wants to be "free." Susan finds herself pregnant at the same time as she learns that her businessman father is coming to take her "home." Allan's family has disintegrated: his overworked father dead, his old-line socialist uncle perennially out of work—all that remains is his stoutly independent mother, working to send him money which he resents taking. More of a statement than a plot, the play ends with Allan's "determination for a reckoning with society for making him an outcast."

Typically, this moment is shown by a close-up of Allan on a screen, and preceded by the chorus "dancing away into a non-landscape of water, sky and earth"—for in this play Ryga has expanded further his use of theatrical devices. Borrowing generously from the multi-media techniques of the new generation itself, he instructs the cast to enter through the audience, and invites the onlookers to join in the closing dance. Film and still projections mix with, and play counterpoint to, the live action onstage. Songs and dances increase in number and variety, and the imaginative interplay of dream and reality becomes less defined; the form becomes musical—a fantasia of themes and variations. The basic Ryga concerns are still there: home, identity, freedom, law, the abuse of human dignity. But here he lays more stress on his impatience with words and with art for art's sake: the opt-out painter becomes, at the end, a social activist.

Now it is hard for a playwright to maintain the ineffectiveness of words, let alone art as a whole—especially if he is a playwright with a message. For the cut and thrust of argument no better medium than words has been invented, and to make a play entertaining one needs all the art one can muster. This appears to have been the problem confronting Ryga when he tackled his next play, *Captives of The Faceless Drummer* (1971), the form of which is essentially a bitter argument between a kidnapped Canadian diplomat and his tough proletarian captor—a disguised replay of the recent terrorist crisis in Quebec. Music and dance, two of the alternatives to words, are not well designed for the conveying of information, and film is obviously a better medium than theatre for the presentation of non-verbal information. But theatre can use words *and* music *and* dance to achieve a combined impact denied any one of them separately, and beyond the power of the mechanical film; they meet on the level of poetic symbolism—a level on which Ryga has always felt comfortable. The use of these other arts to fortify the emotional impact of an otherwise wordy didactic play was being explored in Europe by Peter Weiss, among others—and this was the solution also found by Ryga.

Harry is the cultivated diplomat kidnapped as hostage for a number of imprisoned terrorists. His chief captor, known only as The Commander, is a fibrous, shamelessly uneducated young revolutionary. Mutually trapped in the hide-out by reconnoitering troops, the two men strip each other intellectually and morally—while the outside world, represented by a multipurpose chorus and by Harry's wife, mistress and best friend, swirls around them. Scenes from memory and imagination are played out as they talk; but instead of co-mingling the actors, real and imagined, Ryga here keeps Harry penned in his room while the other characters can come no closer than "an invisible barrier of memory." Adrienne, the wife, personifies (once again) the liberal do-gooder; Jenny, the mistress, is victimized innocence; Fritz, the doctor-friend, is the scared realist who goes by the conventional rule-book. Once again, none of them has a real "home" to go to; and the only one of the lot who knows who he is is the Commander, who is shot at the play's end.

The chorus here is used much more variously than in the earlier plays: breaking into particular roles (Student, Worker, Businessman), giving out statistics ("Taxation is increasing 7% this coming winter!"), illustrating the emotions of the principal characters (". . . strutting confidence that all goes well with Harry"), or even responding to the action like an onstage audience. Such broad and interwoven use of a chorus throughout a play presents the director with a dangerous choice: he has both an invitation to clarify and a temptation to complicate the action—and the further an author moves away from dialogue toward scenarios for choreography, the more he is at the mercy of his director. The balance between movement and speech, between the emotional and the rational elements, becomes acute and precarious in this play, and at a price: the almost continuous sound and action leave little room for the verbal wit which now and then might have relieved the unrelenting tension, and thus reinforced it.

We may expect more plays from George Ryga, with more dramatic experiments. But the most interesting question for the future is one he himself puts in the mouth of the artist Allan in *Grass and Wild Strawberries*: "What have we gained, when a successful revolution becomes establishment the moment it succeeds? " Because Ryga is in grave danger of becoming an established Canadian playwright. In the preface to *Indian,* his first play, he wrote that with it he "won a freedom in form and content which I felt at the time to be unique in Canadian theatrical and television literature"; but for the intervention of a sympathetic producer, he says, *"Indian* would have been an unknown unproduced play relegated to non-life by the self-appointed guardians of dramatic art forms whose crowning achievements have been the Stratford Festival of Ontario and the middle-class exercises of the CBC." Eight years later, he says, "the resistance to evolving dramatic language and form to meet the requirements of a people and their distinctive national identity still persists."

George Ryga has done more than any other Canadian dramatist writing in English to break down that resistance. No one knows better than he that the revolution has only begun. "I have had four productions of my work this year in Canada," he said in 1971. "Every one played to sell-out houses and critical acclaim. And yet my position as a Canadian playwright is in a jeopardized situation. There are no breakthroughs yet. Canadian plays are still accepted only as a token gesture. For me, a single film commission would equal all the fees that I have ever earned for all my plays in Canada." An important question for the Canadian theatre is whether Ryga will keep on fighting in the face of so much unrequited success.

EXTRACT FROM *THE ECSTASY OF RITA JOE*
BY GEORGE RYGA

This is the beginning of the play. I have chosen it because here Ryga sets the scene for everything to follow, and shows most clearly the way in which he reveals his story by the use of free association of memories and reality.

A rehearsal photograph of The Playhouse Theatre's production of The Ecstasy of Rita Joe. *From left to right: Henry Ramer as the Judge, August Schellenberg as Jamie, Frances Hyland as Rita Joe and George Ryga as overseer.*

A circular ramp—beginning at floor level stage left and continuing downward below floor level at stage front, then rising and sweeping along stage back at two-foot elevation to disappear in wings of stage left. This ramp dominates the stage by wrapping the central and forward playing area. A short approach ramp, meeting with the main ramp at stage right, expedites entrances from wings of stage right.

The MAGISTRATE'S chair and representation of court desk are situated at stage right, enclosed within the sweep of the ramp. At the foot of the desk is a lip on stage right side. The SINGER sits here, turned away from the focus of the play. Her songs and accompaniment appear almost accidental. She has all the reactions of a white liberal folklorist with a limited concern and understanding of an ethnic dilemma which she touches in the course of her research and work in compiling and writing folk songs. She serves, too, as an alter ego to RITA.

No curtain is used during the play. At the opening, intermission and conclusion of the play, the curtain remains up. Because of this, the onus for isolating scenes from the past and present in RITA JOE's life falls on highlight lighting.

Backstage, a mountain cyclorama is lowered into place. In front of the cyclorama, a darker maze curtain to suggest gloom and confusion, and a cityscape.

House lights and stage work lights remain on. Backstage, cyclorama, and maze curtain are up, revealing wall back of stage, exit doors, etc.

CAST, SINGER enter off stage singly and in pairs from wings, exit doors back of theatre, from auditorium side doors. The entrances are workmanlike and untheatrical. When all the CAST is on stage, they turn to face the audience momentarily. House lights dim.

Cyclorama lowers into place. Maze curtain follows. This creates a sense of compression of stage into the auditorium. Recorded voices are heard in a jumble of mutterings and throat clearings. The MAGISTRATE enters as the CLERK begins:

CLERK: *(recorded)*
This court is in session. All present will rise . . . *(shuffling and scraping of furniture)* . . . Magistrate's Court reconvenes. The court calls Rita Joe to the stand. Rita Joe!

The CAST repeat "Rita Joe, Rita Joe". A POLICEMAN brings on RITA JOE.

MAGISTRATE:
Who is she? Can she speak English?

POLICEMAN:
Yes.

MAGISTRATE:
Then let her speak for herself! *(speaks to the audience firmly and with reason)* To understand life in a given society, one must understand laws of that society. All relationships . . .

CLERK: *(recorded)*
. . . Man to man . . . man to woman . . . man to property . . . man to the state . . .

MAGISTRATE:
. . . are determined and enriched by laws that have grown out of social realities. The quality of the law under which you live and function determines the real quality of the freedom that was yours today.

The rest of the CAST slowly move out.

Your home and your well-being were protected. The roads of the city are open to us. So are the galleries, libraries, the administrative and public buildings. There are buses, trains—going in and coming out. Nobody is a prisoner here.

RITA:
(with humour, almost a sad sigh) The first time I tried to go home I was picked up by some men who gave me five dollars. An' then they arrested me.

The POLICEMAN retreats into shadows. The SINGER crosses down.

MAGISTRATE:
Thousands leave and enter the city every day . . .

78

RITA:

It wasn't true what they said, but nobody'd believe me . . .

SINGER:

(sings as a recitivo searching for a melody)
Will the winds not blow
My words to her
Like the seeds
Of the dandelion?

MAGISTRATE:

(smiles, as at a private joke) Once . . . I saw a little girl in the Cariboo country. It was summer then and she wore only a blouse and skirt. I wonder what she wore in winter?

MURDERERS hover in background, on upper ramp. One whistles, and one lights a cigarette—an action which will be repeated at the end of the play.

RITA:

(moves to him, but hesitates) You look like a good man. Tell them to let me go, please!

MAGISTRATE goes to his podium.

MAGISTRATE:

Our nation is on an economic par with the state of Arkansas . . . we are a developing country, but a buoyant one. Still . . . the summer report of the Economic Council of Canada predicts a reduction in the gross national product unless we utilize our manpower for greater efficiency. Employed, happy people make for a prosperous, happy nation . . .

RITA:

(exultantly) I worked at some jobs, mister!

The MAGISTRATE turns to face RITA JOE. The MURDERERS have gone.

MAGISTRATE:

. . . Gainful employment. Obedience to the law . . .

RITA:

(to the MAGISTRATE) Once I had a job . . . *(He does not relate to her. She is troubled. She talks to the audience.)* . . . Once I had a job in a tire store . . . an' I'd worry about what time my boss would come . . . he was always late . . . and so was everybody. Sometimes I got to thinkin' what would happen if he'd not come. And nobody else would come. And I'd be all day in this big room with no lights on an' the telephone ringing an' people asking for other people that weren't there . . . What would happen?

As she relates her concern she laughs. Towards the end of her dialogue she is so amused by the absurdity of it all she can hardly contain herself.
Lights fade down on MAGISTRATE who broods in his chair as he examines court papers.
Lights up on JAIMIE PAUL approaching on backstage ramp from stage left. He is jubilant, his laughter blending with her laughter. At the sound of his voice, RITA JOE runs to him, to the memory of him.

JAIMIE:

I seen the city today and I seen things today I never knew was there, Rita Joe!

RITA:

(happily) I seen them, too, Jaimie Paul!

He pauses above her, his mood light and childlike.

JAIMIE:

I seen a guy on top of a bridge, talkin' to himself . . . an' lots of people on the beach watchin' harbour seals . . . Kids feed popcorn to seagulls . . . an' I think to myself—boy! Pigeons eat pretty good here!

RITA:

In the morning, Jaimie Paul . . . very early in the morning . . . the air is cold like at home . . .

JAIMIE:

Pretty soon I seen a little woman walkin' a big black dog on a rope . . . dog is mad . . . dog wants a man!

JAMIE PAUL moves to RITA JOE. They embrace.

RITA:
Clouds are red over the city in the morning. Clara Hill says to me if you're real happy . . . the clouds make you forget you're not home . . .

They laugh together. JAIMIE breaks from her. He punctuates his story with wide, sweeping gestures.

JAIMIE:
I start singin' and some hotel windows open. I wave to them, but nobody waves back! They're watchin' me, like I was a harbour seal! *(laughs)* So I stopped singin'!

RITA:
I remember colours, but I've forgot faces already . . .

JAIMIE PAUL looks at her as her mood changes. Faint light on MAGISTRATE brightens.

RITA:
. . . A train whistle is white, with black lines . . . a sick man talkin' is brown like an overcoat with pockets torn an' string showin' . . . a sad woman is a room with the curtains shut . . . .

MAGISTRATE:
Rita Joe?

She becomes sobered, but JAIMIE continues laughing. She nods to the MAGISTRATE, then turns to JAIMIE.

RITA:
Them bastards put me in jail. They're gonna do it again, they said . . . them bastards!

JAIMIE:
Guys who sell newspapers don't see nothin' . . .

RITA:
They drive by me, lookin' . . .

JAIMIE:
I'm gonna be a carpenter!

RITA:

I walk like a stick, tryin' to keep my ass from showin' because I know what they're thinkin' . . . them bastards!

JAIMIE:

I got myself boots an' a new shirt—see!

RITA:

(worried now) I thought their jail was on fire . . . I thought it was burning.

JAIMIE:

Room I got costs me seven bucks a week . . .

RITA:

I can't leave town. Every time I try, they put me in jail.

POLICEMAN enters with file folder.

JAIMIE:

They say it's a pretty good room for seven bucks a week . . .

JAIMIE begins to retreat backwards from her, along ramp to wings of stage left. She is isolated in a pool of light away from the MAGISTRATE and the light isolation between her and JAIMIE deepens, as the scene turns into the courtroom again.

MAGISTRATE:

Vagrancy . . . You are charged with vagrancy.

JAIMIE:

(with enthusiasm, boyishly) First hundred bucks I make, Rita Joe . . . I'm gonna buy a car so I can take you every place!

RITA:

(moves after him) Jaimie!

He retreats, dreamlike, into the wings. The spell of memory between them broken. Pools of light between her and the MAGISTRATE spread and fuse into single light area. She turns to the MAGISTRATE, worried and confused.

MAGISTRATE:
(reading documents in his hand) The charge against you this morning is vagrancy . . .

MAGISTRATE continues studying papers he holds. She looks up at him and shakes her head helplessly, then blurts out to him.

RITA:
I had to spend last night in jail . . . did you know?

MAGISTRATE:
Yes. You were arrested.

RITA:
I didn't know when morning came . . . there was no windows . . . the jail stinks! People in jail stink!

MAGISTRATE:
(indulgently) Are you surprised?

RITA:
I didn't know anybody there . . . People in jail stink like paper that's been in the rain too long. But a jail stinks worse. It stinks of rust . . . an' old hair . . .

MAGISTRATE looks down at her for the first time.

MAGISTRATE:
You . . . are Rita Joe?

She nods quickly. A faint concern shows in his face. He watches her for a long moment.

MAGISTRATE:
I know your face . . . yet . . . it wasn't in this courtroom. Or was it?

RITA:
I don't know . . .

MAGISTRATE:
(pondering) Have you appeared before me in the past year?

83

RITA:
(turns away from him, shrugs) I don't know. I can't remember . . .

The MAGISTRATE throws his head back and laughs, the POLICEMAN joins in.

MAGISTRATE:
You can't remember? Come now . . .

RITA:
(laughing with him and looking to POLICEMAN) I can't remember . . .

MAGISTRATE:
Then I take it you haven't appeared before me. Certainly you and I would remember if you had.

RITA:
(smiling) I don't remember . . .

The MAGISTRATE makes some hurried notes, but he is watching RITA JOE, formulating his next thought.

RITA:
(naively) My sister hitch-hiked home an' she had no trouble like I . . .

MAGISTRATE:
You'll need witnesses, Rita Joe. I'm only giving you eight hours to find witnesses for yourself . . .

RITA:
Jaimie knows . . .

She turns to where JAIMIE had been, but the back of stage is in darkness. The POLICEMAN exits suddenly.

RITA:
Jaimie knew . . .

Her voice trails off pathetically. The MAGISTRATE shrugs and returns to studying his notes.

Afterword

At first glance, it might seem easy to identify two schools among our four playwrights—and there is nothing especially Canadian about these schools: they are to be found in the theatre of every country. Davies and Reaney seem to represent the educated cultural establishment, while Gélinas and Ryga represent the protesting proletariat. The former are sophisticated intellectuals, concerned with myth, symbol, and all the paraphernalia of Art—while the latter are plainer folk, concerned with the "gut-feelings" of Real Life. Both Davies and Reaney, moreover, are members of the powerful Anglo-Saxon majority in Canada, while Gélinas belongs to the French-speaking minority and Ryga is a New Canadian. The first pair find the Canadian scene a comedy, the second find it tragic—"This world," said Horace Walpole, "is a comedy to those that think, a tragedy to those that feel." One might almost speak in Elizabethan terms of "University Wits" on the one hand, and unschooled Shakespeares on the other. Ryga, in fact, speaks scathingly of "the self-appointed guardians" of "middle-class" culture who stand in the way of "the people."

But a closer look will show us that such a facile pigeonholing is seriously misleading. To begin with, it is Reaney along with Ryga who has been most imaginative in experimenting with new stage forms to meet the requirements of today's audiences, while Gélinas and Davies (despite the wide variety of his plays) have worked within more traditional frameworks. The two younger writers dabble much more freely in mixed-media, use radio and television techniques, and liberally lace their plays with songs and dances. Moreover, both Reaney and Ryga are essentially poets; Gélinas has written entirely in prose, and Davies, while he is a brilliant parodist of other poets, uses verses and songs only incidentally in his plays. In an important sense, Davies and Gélinas are both fundamentally comic actors (Davies was a professional actor, Gélinas still is), while both Reaney and Ryga come at their trade from a basically literary/musical point of view.

Even this pairing, however, obscures significant similarities and differences between the quartet. For example, it is Davies who comes closest to Ryga's dissatisfaction with society as it is and determination to change it for something better—while Reaney seems content to mythologize his past and Gélinas to maintain a philosophical stoicism. If Davies wants the artist to be more hospitably owned in Canada, Ryga's complaint that "Canadian plays are still accepted only as a token gesture" amounts to the same thing. If Ryga joins today's societies for the promotion of Canadian playwrights, Davies in his own way fought the good fight twenty years ago as secretary of the Massey Commission, whose recommendations led to the setting up of both federal and provincial arts councils. Both of them, in fact, have been social rebels working for a brighter future—about which Reaney seems unconcerned and Gélinas existentially impartial. Perhaps behind this is the consideration that Davies and Ryga are both first-generation Canadians, while Reaney's forbears arrived in the early nineteenth century, and Gélinas' a century before that. Davies still has umbilical links to his father's Wales and his mother's Scotland, and Ryga to his parents' Ukraine. In *Fortune, My Foe* it is the newcomer Franz Szabo who still has the enthusiasm to want to change his adopted land; those who have been around longer have learned to accept its cruelties. Only after Gélinas painted a realistic picture of his native Quebec did younger writers seize the theatre as a means of improving the lot of its subject.

I must end by pointing out the similarities between all four of these Canadian playwrights. With few exceptions among their works, they have all tried to reach universal truths by digging down into their own roots instead of spreading out to grasp the ready-made truths available from the wholesale markets of Britain, France or the United States. This is doing things the hard way, but the only sure way in the long run. It is perhaps early to judge when and where each has been successful; but it has led all of them to tackle themes which, as often as not, differ from the themes which interest audiences in other larger societies. Whether it be the plight of the Canadian Indian, the temptation of moving to greener fields, the rights of our minority cultures, or coming-of-age in a small-town Ontario, they are dealing fundamentally with "small country" problems, with a search for identity in a world where others more self-confident already know who they are. Even when the themes are seen as universal (suppression, selling one's soul, human rights, growing-up), they are still clothed in what to other audiences must seem like peculiar—and provincial—garments.

The writing of Canadian plays, therefore, is and will continue to be a risky business. But it is worth it—for without an image of ourselves we are nobody, and can never be anybody worth the rest of the world's attention.

Endnote

I have mentioned a number of other Canadian playwrights in this book. If you would like to read their plays, here is a "starter" list:

Herbert, John. *Fortune and Men's Eyes* (New York: Grove Press).

Joudry, Patricia. *Teach Me How to Cry* (New York: Samuel French).

Murphy, Arthur. *The First Falls on Monday* (Toronto: University of Toronto Press).

de la Roche, Mazo. *Whiteoaks* (Toronto: Macmillan).

Coulter, John. *The Trial of Louis Riel* (Ottawa: Oberon Press).

Simons, Beverley. *Crabdance* (Vancouver: Talonplays).

Sinclair, Lister. *The Blood is Strong* (Toronto: Book Society).

Many of the newer playwrights are not yet in print—but here are a few who are:

Freeman, David. *Creeps* (Toronto: University of Toronto Press).

Fruett, Bill: *Wedding in White* (in "A Collection of Canadian Plays," Vol. II, Toronto: Simon & Pierre).

French, David: *Leaving Home* (Toronto: new press).

There are several more plays in "A Collection of Canadian Plays," of which only Volumes I and II have been published so far; and typescripts of more than two hundred plays by Canadian playwrights are available from the Playwrights Co-op, 344 Dupont Street, Toronto 179, Ontario. The Co-op will also send you a catalogue on request.

Brock University, in 1972, published the *Brock Bibliography of Published Canadian Stage Plays in English 1900-1972;* it is available from Brock University, St. Catharines, Ontario. This excellent bibliography is an exciting example of what students can achieve, for it commenced as a project of one class in Dramatic Media. They formed a research team which acquired an Opportunities for Youth grant and produced this valuable list of almost nine hundred titles.

Several French plays newly available in English translation are:

> Dubé, Marcel. *The White Geese* (Toronto: new press, 1972).
>
> Dufresne, Guy. *Call of the Whippoorwill* (Toronto: new press, 1972).
>
> Gurik, Robert. *The Hanged Man* (Toronto: new press, 1972).
>
> Tremblay, Michel. *Ta Marie-Lou* (Toronto: new press, 1973).

But if you read French and would like to know more about Quebec writers and their plays, consult *Le Théâtre Québecois* by Jean-Cléo Godin and Laurent Mailhot, published by Editions HMH, Ltée, Montreal. The best history of Quebec theatre is Jean Béraud's *350 ans de théâtre au Canada français* (published in Montreal by Le Cercle du livre de France)—but it is unfortunately not yet available in English.

No general history of English-speaking theatre in Canada has yet been published, although one or two have been promised. You can, however, get an excellent idea of much of it (Eastern Canada from 1790 to 1914) from Murray Edwards' *A Stage in Our Past* (Toronto: University of Toronto Press), which also contains titles and synopses of many early Canadian plays in which you may be interested. Professor Edwards includes a most useful bibliography of historical sources.

Finally, although few theatrical reference works emanating from either Britain or the United States allude to the theatre in Canada, the latest (1967) edition of *The Oxford Companion to the Theatre* has (under the heading "Canada") a generally accurate brief history of both English and French-language stages, companies, performers and playwrights.

If you happen to be interested in themes and ideas in Canadian literature generally— including dramatic literature—see Margaret Atwood's *Survival,* Toronto: House of Anansi, 1972.

Selected Bibliography

ROBERTSON DAVIES

PLAYS:

Eros at Breakfast & Other Plays. Toronto: Clarke, Irwin & Co. Ltd., 1949.
Fortune, My Foe. Toronto: Clarke, Irwin & Co. Ltd., 1949.
At My Heart's Core. Toronto: Clarke, Irwin & Co. Ltd., 1950.
A Mask of Aesop. Toronto: Clarke, Irwin & Co. Ltd., 1952.
A Jig for the Gypsy. Toronto: Clarke, Irwin & Co. Ltd., 1954.
A Masque for Mr. Punch. Toronto: Clarke, Irwin & Co. Ltd., 1954.
Hunting Stuart and Other Plays, ed. B. Parker (incl. *King Phoenix, Hunting Stuart, General Confession*). Toronto: new press, 1972.

COMMENTARY:

Buitenhuis, E. *Robertson Davies* (Canadian Writers & Their Works). Toronto: Forum House, 1972.
Steinberg, M.W., "Don Quixote and the Puppets: Theme and Structure in Robertson Davies' Drama," *Canadian Literature,* VII (Winter, 1961).

90

GRATIEN GELINAS

PLAYS (in English translation):

Tit-Coq, trans. Kenneth Johnstone. Toronto: Clarke, Irwin
& Co. Ltd., 1950.
Bousille and the Just, trans. Kenneth Johnstone. Toronto:
Clarke, Irwin & Co. Ltd., 1961.
Yesterday the Children Were Dancing, trans. Mavor Moore.
Toronto: Clarke, Irwin & Co. Ltd., 1967.

COMMENTARY:

Godin, J.-C., and Mailhot, L. *Le Théâtre Québécois.*
Montréal: Editions HMH Ltée., 1970. (In French.)
Ross, M., ed., *The Arts in Canada.* Toronto: Macmillan,
1958. (Béraud, J.: "Theatre in French-Canada." French
with English Translation.)

JAMES REANEY

PLAYS:

*The Killdeer & Other Plays (The Killdeer (I), The Sun and
the Moon, One-Man Masque, Night Blooming Cereus).*
Toronto: Macmillan, 1962.
Colours in the Dark. Talonplays (Vancouver) with
Macmillan, 1969.
Listen to the Wind. Talonplays (Vancouver) with Macmillan,
1971.
Names & Nicknames & Other Plays for Young People.
Talonplays (Vancouver) with Macmillan, 1972.
Masks of Childhood, ed. Parker (including *The Easter Egg,
Three Desks, The Killdeer (II).* Toronto: new press, 1972.

COMMENTARY:

Lee, A.A. *James Reaney.* New York: Twayne Publishers,
Inc., 1968.
Woodman, R.G. *James Reaney* (Canadian Writers No. 12).
Toronto: McClelland and Stewart Ltd., 1971.

GEORGE RYGA

PLAYS:

The Ecstasy of Rita Joe and Other Plays, ed. B. Parker
(includes *Indian, The Ecstasy of Rita Joe, Grass and Wild
Strawberries).* Toronto: new press, 1971.
Captives of the Faceless Drummer. Vancouver: Talonplays, 1971.

COMMENTARY:

Parker, B. Introduction to *The Ecstasy of Rita Joe and
Other Plays.* Toronto: new press, 1971.